Central Park

An American Masterpiece

Central Park

AN AMERICAN MASTERPIECE

Text and Photographs by Sara Cedar Miller

Harry N. Abrams, Inc., Publishers, in association with the Central Park Conservancy

To Alison Miller, Kevin Kiddoo, and Samuel Cedar because "Knowledge is Good" and so is love

Contents

From 180 miles above the earth's surface, astronauts can view Central Park
from space with the naked eye.
Commander Curt Brown of the NASA
shuttle Discovery commented,
"Central Park is right there, a nice
green spot in the middle of the city."

Preface By Kenneth T. Jackson

Central Park is not the oldest public open space in either the world or in the United States. After all, Tiananmen Square in Beijing and the Piazza San Marco in Venice, among many others, had been attracting visitors centuries before Christopher Columbus found his way to the New World. And on the North American continent, one might think of the Boston Common, or the many squares that William Penn laid out for Philadelphia, or the small open spaces in Savannah as areas where the city fathers thought to give the citizenry an opportunity to breathe and to enjoy nature's bounty even as they put in streets and sold building lots to meet economic requirements. By that calculation, the great central park in New York City is a relative newcomer, its birthday reckoned by most scholars as no earlier than 1853.

Similarly, Central Park is not the largest green oasis in the boundaries of a large city. The United States alone offers many examples of urban reservations that are many times the size of Frederick Law Olmsted and Calvert Vaux's Manhattan creation. Indeed, Central Park does not even rank as number one in the city that is its home. Van Cortlandt Park in the Bronx and the Gateway National Recreation Area in Queens both encompass many more acres.

Finally, Central Park is not the most beautiful public open space on the planet. Each American city might put forward a park that might claim such a title; Olmsted and Vaux themselves pointed to Prospect Park in Brooklyn as being rather more pleasing to the eye and the imagination.

But Central Park is the most important public space in the United States. Prior to the acceptance of the Greensward Plan in 1858, no American city provided large open areas for public relaxation, partly because the poor conceived of parks as aristocratic preserves where royalty rode to the hounds, and partly because the rich thought of parks as refuges for idlers and hoboes. There were attractive parks in London, Paris, Copenhagen, and other European capitals, but those spaces had originally been assembled for monarchs and their invited guests. What made Central Park different was the fact that it was the first grand open space that had been intentionally set aside for the ordinary public in a prosperous and ambitious city. Even before it opened it attracted millions of visitors, and it seemed to pay for itself through the increased value of the real estate that surrounded it.

Twenty years under construction, Central Park required the labor of thousands of men to dig out its ponds and to build up its hills. Soon enough, however, it was renowned as an island of solitude in the midst of a throbbing metropolis. And after Central Park opened to such fanfare and acclaim in Manhattan, no city in America that thought well of its future could afford not to build a similar amenity. After all, if the largest and richest agglomeration in the nation could set aside 843 acres for public use, what excuse could Memphis or Kansas City or Baltimore or a hundred other cities offer for not also building a great park?

Central Park did not satisfy every critic or every demand. Because the poor tended to live many miles away, its footpaths and walkways were more accessible, then as now, to the middle and upper classes than to the slum families that needed them the most. And amenities such as swings and seesaws were not initially allowed; the Olmsted and Vaux idea was rather to commune with nature and to provide a place where persons of all classes and conditions could come together for enrichment and regeneration. In Manhattan, moreover, where average residential densities could exceed 100,000 per square mile even before the Civil War, the need for breathing space was not met even by Central Park.

Vaux worked intermittently on Central Park for the rest of his life. However, in the late 1870s, Olmsted became increasingly frustrated and disillusioned by what he saw as venal politicians, rapacious businessmen, and by the degree to which his theories and solutions failed to win broad acceptance. Despite important public commissions in Louisville, Detroit, Boston, Chicago, and Rochester, he retreated for much of the remainder of his long life to a private practice for millionaires—the huge Biltmore domain of George Vanderbilt in North Carolina was a good example—in which aesthetic rather than social concerns were emphasized. But the deed had been done, the example had been set. American cities would brag about their beautiful open spaces for generations to come, which is the most powerful endorsement of the example of New York City's Central Park.

Kenneth T. Jackson is the president of the New-York Historical Society and the Jacques Barzun Professor of History and the Social Sciences at Columbia University.

Landscapes are culture before they are nature; constructs of the imagination projected onto wood and water and rock.[1]

—SIMON SCHAMA

Central Park is the most important work of American art of the nineteenth century. In the visual arts, no single painting, sculpture, or structure can compare with this unique and long-recognized masterpiece of landscape architecture. In the late 1960s environmental artists, who shaped the land into massive compositions, recognized the groundbreaking status of Central Park as a new art form—America's first earthwork. Robert Smithson,

a spokesman for the movement and creator of its most iconic piece, *Spiral Jetty*, identified one of the Park's codesigners, Frederick Law Olmsted, as "America's first 'earthwork artist,'" and viewed the magnitude of his creation as a work that "throws a whole new light on the nature of American art."[2]

The environmental art movement of the 1960s grew out of dissatisfaction with the traditional picture-in-a-frame, sculpture-on-a-pedestal status of art. A century earlier, Frederick Law Olmsted and his partner, Calvert Vaux (rhymes with "rocks"), fought to establish themselves as artists

and to equate their work with the venerable tradition of landscape painting. Olmsted, the spokesman for the partnership, identified himself as a visual artist in his explanation of the complexity of his creative process:

> *The work of design necessarily supposes a gallery of mental pictures, and in all parts of the Park . . . a picture which as Superintendent I am constantly laboring to realize . . . I shall venture to assume to myself the title of artist and to add that no sculptor, painter or architect can have anything like the difficulty in sketching and conveying a knowledge of his design.*[3]

One year later, the board of commissioners of Central Park validated Olmsted's artistic intent, proudly declaring, "The Park has attractions to those that visit it merely as a picture . . . the eye is gratified at the picture, that constantly changes with the movement of the observer."[4] Ten years later, when the Park was near completion, Olmsted affirmed its status as a work of art—a declaration that has since become its guiding principle:

> *The Park throughout is a single work of art, and as subject to the primary law of every work of art, namely that it shall be framed upon a single, noble motive, to which the design of all its parts, in some more or less subtle way, shall be confluent and helpful.*[5]

Central Park is the living embodiment of nineteenth-century American landscape paintings, particularly those of the Hudson River, or New York, School. Those paintings were the attempt of a restless age to create a bold, new art that would, in the words of painter Worthington Whittredge on his return from a European trip in 1859, "distinguish it from the art of the other nations and to enable us to pronounce without shame the oft repeated phrase, 'American Art.'"[6]

Whittredge and his contemporary artists in antebellum America were searching their collective soul for an art rooted in their national soil, an indigenous art to equal the grand European traditions. The traditional source of American pride—its uniquely democratic government—was at risk in the years before the Civil War, and the country needed to rally around a theme that would unify a divided nation. Common ground was found literally in the ground itself. Americans realized that their spectacular *natural* resources were their greatest *national* resources.

No longer did Americans have to feel ashamed that they did not possess the ancient monuments of Greece or Rome or the national treasures of England, France, or Italy. A continent of vast mountains, deep canyons, and thundering cascades was deemed more venerable and majestic than anything made by Europeans. Even an Egyptian pyramid could not hold a candle to the nobility of Niagara Falls. The celebration of America's natural history would far surpass Europe's cultural history and take center stage as the new subject for American paintings.

Taming the Land

While social and political problems loomed over the country, Americans could always boast of their successful dominion over the continent itself. When the Pilgrims first landed in Plymouth in 1620, the wildness of the unfamiliar terrain seemed threatening and intimidating. Quickly, however, the new settlers tamed the "remote, rocky, barren, bushy, wild, woody wilderness" so it resembled the familiar geography of their native country, and, by 1653, colonist Edward Johnson called his new land "a second England for fertileness."[7]

By the mid-nineteenth century, taming the land had become an integral part of the national purpose. Dynamic technologies such as railroads, telegraph cables, and canals gave Americans a new sense of mastery over the breadth of their continent, including its indigenous peoples and wildlife. Americans pursued a national identity and unity by controlling the land. Congress seized the land in the name of manifest destiny, and artists captured it on rectangles of film and canvas.

In her convincing analysis of American landscape paintings of the antebellum period, Angela Miller has argued

It is easy to forget that the Park, composed of trees, water, and rock, is as much a man-made creation as the buildings that face it.

that these works of art imposed aesthetically pleasing order and structure on the untamed wilderness, "a metaphor or symbolic substitute for other, more elusive forms of social and cultural unity."[8] Controlling the land was easier on canvas than taming the "qualities of real nature, its accidents of topography, its signs of cataclysm and geological change," a feat that Miller explains was "impossible to engineer in reality."[9] What Miller overlooked, however, was the creation of Central Park—an entirely new, engineered form of art.

A Man-Made Landscape

Many people assume that the Park is the last remaining tract of Manhattan's natural land forms. Horace Greeley, the famous newspaper editor, went to the Park shortly after it was opened and exclaimed "Well they have let it alone better than I thought they would."[10] Greeley was entirely wrong.

Central Park in the 1850s was America's greatest example of the marriage of aesthetics and engineering. In this, it has always been a glorious paradox: above ground it is a designed landscape that copies nature so closely that it disguises its own fabrication and, below ground, it is an efficient technological system.

Unlike European culture, which made great distinction between the fine arts and technological innovation,

Top: All of the Park's water bodies were originally swamps, such as the Pond on 59th Street, photographed before construction began in 1857.

Middle and bottom: Water is fed into the Pond through the stormwater system and is augmented with water from the city water supply. The seemingly natural outflow is, in reality, a concrete spillway that controls the elevation of water. The reinforced concrete structure is camouflaged beneath artfully placed boulders. Below the shrubs and ground cover that grow along the shore of the Pond is an engineered slope. Constructed of controlled fill and a geosynthetic clay liner, it is reinforced with other high-tech products to ensure stability of the steep slope and keep the Pond watertight. Aquatic plants grow on constructed shelves that line the shore of the Pond.

Americans prided themselves on blurring the line between the two. Like every machine and every work of art, Central Park is entirely man-made. The broad meadows were created from blasting the outcrops, draining the swamps, and filling them with tens of thousands of cartloads of soil. The naturalistic lakes were the result of water flowing through the same system of pipes that also filled the bathtubs and kitchen sinks of well-to-do New Yorkers.[11]

The 843-acre Park *seems* natural because it is composed of real soil, grass, trees, water, and flowers that need constant tending. In reality, however, it is naturalistic—an engineered environment that is closer in essence to scenes created in Hollywood than it is to the creation of Mother Nature. In discussing his design, Olmsted admitted to the necessity of "undignified tricks of disguise, or mere affectations of rusticity" in order to reach the sought-after effects of "simplicity, tranquility and unsophisticated naturalness" found in the rural landscapes and the paintings that he and his codesigner, Calvert Vaux, sought to emulate.[12]

Like most complex works of art, Central Park is greater than the sum of its parts. Through its landscapes, architecture, and sculpture, we will discover why Central Park deserves to be considered the most important work of American art of the nineteenth century.

"Chapter 1: An Under- and Overview," a survey of seven diverse features of the nineteenth-century Park, provides a broad overview of the Park's underlying sociocultural meanings and a below-ground view of the technological innovations that make the Park such a unique and innovative work of art.

"Chapter 2: The Heart of the Park" reveals Bethesda Terrace as the defining landscape of Central Park, a masterpiece-within-the-masterpiece that reflects the predominant scientific theories, political concerns, and artistic philosophies of mid-nineteenth-century America.

"Chapter 3: Kindred Spirits" traces the evolution of the park concept through the relationships of its most influential people, while shedding new light on the original design of America's first urban park. In addition to the three well-known entries to the 1858 design competition—those of engineers Egbert Viele and George Waring and the winning "Greensward" plan by Calvert Vaux and Frederick Law Olmsted—two previously unpublished submissions will be discussed, one by engineer John J. Rink and the other—the second prize—by the first superintendent of planting, Samuel Gustin.

"Chapter 4: The Landscapes" charts the development of the design from winning entry to constructed work of art. This chapter explores how the landscapes and features of the Park took shape and how several elements from other competition entries were adapted into the Greensward plan. It also shows how the persistence of two influential commissioners, August Belmont and Robert Dillon, shifted the design from the singular vision of Olmsted and Vaux to a design that was the result of political compromises commonly made in a democratic society.

"Chapter 5: The Architecture" discusses the structures and buildings in the Park and their connection to its larger artistic and social visions. Olmsted and Vaux preferred that the landscapes dominate and created buildings that complemented them. Later, during the 1870–71 administration of William M. "Boss" Tweed, the function and purpose of the Park were broadened by the addition of buildings, attractions, and cultural institutions, echoing the publicly driven design process discussed in Chapter 4.

"Chapter 6: The Sculpture" discusses the important role that sculptures and monuments play in defining the Park as a democratic work of art. The Park's sculptures may be appreciated on several levels: as individual works, in relationship to their respective sites, and in their contribution to the evolving function of the Park. The collection of monuments in Central Park is representative of the most important sculptors and stylistic movements of nineteenth- and twentieth-century American art and commemorates most of the important political events and landmarks in American history.

"Epilogue," by Elizabeth Barlow Rogers, briefly explains the watershed role that Central Park played in the further development of urban parks throughout the country, contributing to its premier status as the most influential artwork of nineteenth-century America.

The meaning of Central Park—its celebration of democracy, technology, nature, and popular culture—is written in its stones and reflected in its waters. Much of the original technological innovation and symbolic decoration of the Park would have been appreciated by and recognizable to a nineteenth-century visitor, since both the Park and its visitors were products of a common American culture. But twenty-first-century visitors— while we readily relate to aspects of the Park introduced in our own time,

such as Strawberry Fields or the statue of Duke Ellington—are less likely to appreciate the significance and the novelty of the original meaning of certain Park features, from which we are separated by a century and a half. Chapters 1 and 2 will examine eight of these original features and uncover their underlying meanings through a tour, beginning at the 60th Street entrance and proceeding to Bethesda Terrace, "the heart of the Park," at 72nd Street. We begin where all visitors to the Park begin—at the gates.

AMERICAN VIEWS.

Central
Park
N.Y.

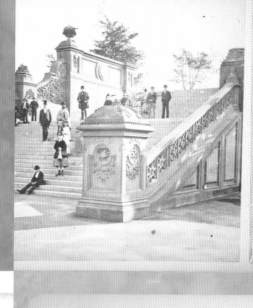

American Scenery.

Central Park,

AMERICAN VIEWS.

Central Park

Central Park, N. Y.

10570. The Terrace.

AMERICAN VIEWS.

Central Park, New York,

CENTRAL PARK.

Most visitors today pass through the entrances or "gates" to Central Park without realizing that they are sermons in stone, proselytizing important cultural values of mid-nineteenth-century New York. Most of these breaks in the simple stone wall surrounding the Park bear the inscription of a calling, such as "Scholars' Gate," or of a specific profession, such as "Mariners' Gate."[1] These rarely used names were meant, on the most basic level, to provide Park visitors with a clear and simple way to arrange a rendezvous. Seeking a "brief, apt, and convenient" naming system for the gates, the commissioners dismissed the numbering system of the city streets as "unsuitable for Park use." The very purpose of the romantic landscape, featuring curvilinear drives and meandering paths, they reasoned, was to escape New York's unrelenting grid. Arranging to meet at 60th and Fifth, for example, only called attention to the urban life that the designers wanted visitors to forget during their time in the Park. Instead, the commissioners sought a "simple and comprehensive system" intrinsic to the Park itself. After rejecting many ideas—references to war victories, the names of the states, important cities in the Union, or names of prominent men—they suggested naming the gates after the workers who made New York City the great metropolis that it had become.[2]

The system incorporates both skilled and unskilled professions into four main categories, which are represented at the entrances along 59th Street: Scholars (at Fifth Avenue), Artists (at Sixth Avenue), Artizans [sic] (at Seventh Avenue), and Merchants (at Broadway/Eighth Avenue). Nine of the other eighteen gates honor occupations that were impor-

Opposite: The nineteenth-century Park.
Above: The names of the eighteen original gates to the Park
emphasized important cultural values to early visitors.

tant in New York history: Pioneers, Farmers, Hunters, Miners, Woodsmen, Mariners, Engineers, Inventors, and Warriors (soldiers).

The gates thus named target the value of honest toil and the Protestant work ethic that have always been defining characteristics and fundamental elements of the American way of life. The conviction that business comes first was important to the founders of America. New England Puritans, French Huguenots, Pennsylvania Quakers, and Swiss and Dutch Calvinists all believed that God would grant eternal life to those who displayed diligence at work, scrupulous use of time, and the deferment of pleasure. Gainful employment and hard work would eventually assure acceptance into heaven, but until that day those industrious New Yorkers could at least merit passage through the gates of their city's earthly paradise.

Even "[h]eaven itself will be dull and stupid" it was thought, "if there is no work to be done in it—nothing to struggle for—[and] no chance to make an improvement."[3] This attitude, described by Frederick Law Olmsted for an 1853 article in the *New-York Daily Times,* not only characterized Americans in general but more specifically defined the core of a Northerner. Naming the gates after professions and occupations, therefore, also reflected the commissioners' support of the North's free labor system over the slave system of the South—the conflict that was tearing the nation in two during the creation and construction of Central Park. The Northerner, Olmsted felt, "finds happiness in doing. Rest, in itself, is irksome and offensive to him." On the other hand, Olmsted characterized the Southerner as having "less curiosity . . . less originating genius, less inventive talent, less patient and persevering energy," being one who is "habitually leaving all matters . . . to his slaves."[4] A walk through the gates, then, was a reminder to visitors that they were not entering a slave plantation but rather a free public park that was created and maintained by paid labor.

The commissioners emphasized that a visit through the gates of Central Park was an earned reward:

> *While the Park is intended as a place for freedom and relaxation, for play and not for work, it has been constructed with no idea of encouraging habits of laziness, or in any way for the benefit of idlers and drones . . . its paramount object is to offer facilities for a daily enjoyment of life to the industrious thousands who are working steadily and conscientiously.*[5]

This proviso reflected not only their deep-seated religious and economic beliefs, but also their need to control an unsettling social climate that had been developing since the 1830s. At that time, an influx of people began to radically alter the city's demographics. The old agrarian lifestyle of Jeffersonian America was being replaced by an urban industrial society, which attracted rural farm workers to cities in search of new jobs and new opportunities. Displaced African Americans, freed by emancipation, manumission, or migration arrived in New York and other American cities with no education, skills, or support.

Foreign immigrants joined these rural migrants and former farmhands. By the middle of the nineteenth-century New York was a city of almost seven hundred thousand people—the most populous city in the Western Hemisphere—and by 1855 more than half the population was foreign-born. Germans were among the first to arrive, drawn to America in 1848 due to political revolution and turbulence in their native land. The largest group of all, the Irish, arrived with massive problems. Starving from the devastating potato famine, they were sick, penniless, uneducated, and unskilled. Many new settlers lived in overcrowded tenements in the Five Points section of town, now the area behind the courthouses on Centre Street. Illness and death were rampant. In 1856 deaths exceeded births, two-thirds of the dead being poor children under the age of six.[6] The Irish had no friends and few sanctuaries. The church, their angel of mercy in Ireland, was underfunded and overwhelmed in New York. Worst of all, the Irish practiced either Roman Catholicism or pagan Celtic rituals, both despised in Protestant America, making life even harder for them.[7]

This influx of new faces, cultures, and diseases made the old New York establishment feel like strangers in a strange land. Well-to-do and middle-class residents fled downtown as never before into newly formed, exclusive neighborhoods of single-family houses further uptown. Socializing occurred in the home; when outside, even middle-class New Yorkers traveled in the protective confines of private carriages and frequented privately controlled spaces: theaters, lecture halls, exhibition halls, and fee-paying gardens and pleasure grounds. Needless to say, the idea of a public park inviting the democratic integration of all people was not immediately welcomed. The Battery, a park situated at the tip of the island, was initially quite popular with genteel society, but when "loafers" and immigrants arrived, they abandoned it.

The few green spaces that were created in the early nineteenth century, such as St. John's Park and Gramercy Park, were gated and available only to owners of the adjacent homes. In 1851 Andrew Jackson Downing, America's foremost landscape designer and tastemaker, published "The New-York Park" in his *Horticulturist* magazine, urging New Yorkers to "Plant spacious parks in your cities, and unloose the gates as wide as the gates of morning to the whole people."[8] One year later, Downing died, but his young English-born partner, Calvert Vaux, would soon hold the key to open those locked gates forever.

During the antebellum years feelings of national pride became both fused and confused with regional and local concerns. On one hand, New Yorkers boasted of their financial and cultural leadership of the Union; on the other, they also saw themselves as superior to both South and North. Soon after the founding fathers revoked the decision to make New York the political capital of the United States in 1789, the proud New York elite resolved instead to make the city the financial and artistic center of the nation. They would be a part of America while also being apart from it. They would work the hardest, become the richest, and enjoy the best. It was assumed that "the best" was on a par with the cultural refinement of the great European capitals London, Paris, and Rome. Though New York could boast neither ancient ruins nor medieval castles nor cathedrals, it could acquire great libraries and art collections and build impressive structures in which to house them. The city could also have a large and beautiful park.

The civic and business leaders of New York knew that a park was a defining characteristic of sophistication and culture. All the great cities of Europe had spacious public parks: London had Hyde Park, Regent's Park, and St. James Park; Paris had the Tuilleries, the Jardin du Luxembourg, and the newly redesigned Bois de Boulogne. These parks had originally been properties of the crown, which had given the grounds over to the public beginning in the eighteenth century. Some New Yorkers asked themselves why these former monarchies did more for their subjects than their own republican form of government.

After much political maneuvering, on July 21, 1853, the New York State Legislature enacted into law the setting aside of more than 750 acres of land central to Manhattan Island to create America's first major landscaped park; they would soon refer to it as "the Central Park."[9] The Park commissioners in their 1862 report on the nomenclature of the gates would applaud New York's civic wisdom, its industriousness, and its ensuing wealth as the qualities that created the Park:

> The construction of the Park has been easily achieved, because the industrious population of New York has been wise enough to require it, and rich enough to pay for it: to New Yorkers it belongs wholly, and these . . . gateways may, perhaps, be allowed to recognize this proprietary right, and to extend to each citizen a respectful welcome.[10]

"A respectful welcome" to the full gamut of society developed slowly. There was no precedent for a government-built public park, and many were doubtful that such an experiment in democracy could be successful. Even as the land for the Park was being cleared in 1857, the intermingling of genteel society with the inhabitants of the Five Points slums seemed abhorrent to many New Yorkers.

> As long as we are governed by the Five Points, our best attempts at elegance and grace will bear some resemblance to jewels in the snouts of swine. Rather the Park should never be made at all if it is to become the resort of rapscalians.[11]

Nonetheless, visionary reformers throughout the city committed themselves to the democratic principles upon which America was founded. And while political activists fought for equality through grass-roots legislation, social visionaries—Vaux and Olmsted among them—would see democracy's greatest potential in the grass itself. Just as it does today, the Park would provide an equal opportunity for a free and healthy natural environment for those who could afford neither the time nor the money for an excursion into the country. Most middle-class people worked six days a week and most poor people, if they were lucky to work at all, worked every day. Frederick Law Olmsted stated this primary mission of Central Park:

> It is one great purpose of the Park to supply to the hundreds and thousands of tired workers, who have no opportunity to spend their summers in the country, a specimen of God's handiwork that shall be to them, inexpensively, what a month or two in the White Mountains or the Adirondacks is, at great cost, to those in easier circumstances.[12]

In 1857, the commissioners of Central Park held a competition for its design. As no major public park had been previously built in an American city, most entrants turned to European models, such as the Bois de Boulogne, for design prototypes. The major entranceway at Scholars' Gate imitated the Avenue de l'Impératrice, the mile-long roadway to the newly constructed Bois de Boulogne in Paris, which featured three separate and parallel types of paths: a pedestrian walkway, a carriage drive, and a bridle trail. These three roads ensured that those engaged in each mode of transportation would have the ability to regard each other without the danger of mixing traffic. Constant perils prevailed in the congested downtown streets, and the elimination of those dangers through the use of separate lanes provided visitors with unprecedented psychological relief.

The expense of owning a pleasure vehicle or a horse for recreational riding also tended by default to separate Park visitors into different socioeconomic groups, as the well-to-do were in carriages or on horseback and the poorer working classes were on foot. The design itself did not purposely intend to reinforce class division but, nonetheless, it echoed the social situation that had already been established on the streets of New York. Recognizing the popular fascination with watching the lifestyles of the rich, Olmsted and Vaux placed their pedestrian paths parallel to the carriage road. "As a general rule," the designers wrote in their plan,

> we propose to run footpaths, close to the carriage roads . . . it is hardly thought that any plan would be popular in New York, that did not allow of a continuous promenade along the drives, so that pedestrians may have ample opportunity to look at the equipages and their inmates. [13]

Strolling on the pathways is still the most popular Park activity. While horse-drawn carriages are a famous tourist attraction, the drives are now used for biking, rollerblading, and jogging—activities unthinkable in the nineteenth century.

Olmsted and other social reformers of the day firmly believed that "the poor need[ed] an education to the refinement and tastes and the mental & moral capital of gentlemen."[14] By 1870 Olmsted boasted that the Park "exercises a distinctly harmonizing and refining influence upon the most unfortunate and most lawless classes of the city,—an influence favorable to courtesy, self-control, and temperance."[15] To Olmsted, Vaux, and their group of gentleman reformers, people-watching in the Park could help an individual become a virtuous and orderly member of bourgeois society. The Park would provide common ground—particularly on the shared pedestrian paths—on which the interaction of the classes would improve civility and inculcate socially acceptable behavior. Toward this grand aspiration of design, Central Park provided the pathways to the American dream.

Left: Maurice Prendergast, Central Park, 1914–15. People-watching has always been one of the most important functions of Central Park. The pedestrian paths were placed alongside the carriage drives and bridle trail so gregarious New Yorkers could watch the parade of wealthy riders on horseback and in their lavish carriages.

Below: John Bachman, Central Park, Bird's Eye View, lithograph, 1863. The design of the Park was created as a tapestry of varying scenes of breathtaking beauty to be experienced on pedestrian pathways, bridle trails, and carriage drives. Today visitors use the system to experience the Park's restored beauty.

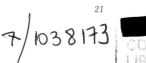

Initially, the gates of the Park were intended to be decorated with statues that reflected the respective professions so that, whether entering on the paths or the trails, visitors would receive an education in history. One of the most important functions of Central Park, catering as it did to many immigrants who often spoke or read no English, was to inculcate in them a sense of national unity and pride. Sculptures were the textbooks in this democratic classroom, and they were "read" as tangible reflections of America's social, political, and cultural history. Statues of notable American figures such as *General William Tecumseh Sherman* (1903) placed just outside the entrance to Scholars' Gate, the Civil War soldier of the *Seventh Regiment Memorial* (1874), *Daniel Webster* (1876), *Alexander Hamilton* (1880), and *The Pilgrim* (1885) made the country's founding fathers, patriots, and heroes available to the foreign-born or uneducated public. As one American stated in 1846, monuments "bring before us in our daily walks the idea of country in a visible shape."[16]

Conversely, newly arriving ethnic groups began to place statues of their folk heroes, cultural leaders, and political figures in Central Park. From 1869 until 1982, for example, Park visitors would have encountered the bust of *Alexander von Humboldt,* the most popular and famous intellectual of the nineteenth century, which was appropriately placed at the Scholars' Gate.[17] It was donated to the Park by a group

of German Americans who wished to memorialize the centennial of their countryman's birth. For the first time in this country, various groups could congregate in a public space and pay homage to the heroes of their Old World culture. This kind of *Volksgarten* had been a common sight in

German parks, but the sculptures in those parks honored people from the same ethnic group or national origin. Central Park, on the other hand, became the first showcase for monuments representing a wide range of nationalities.

In 1859, German Americans donated the bust of poet and dramatist *Johann Christoph Fredrich von Schiller,* the first sculpture to be placed in the new Park, followed by *Alexander von Humboldt* and *Ludwig van Beethoven.* Other ethnic groups soon followed in making contributions of monuments: Irish poet *Thomas Moore,* Scottish writers *Sir Walter Scott* and *Robert Burns,* Italian politician *Giuseppe Mazzini,* and the Italian-born *Christoforo Columbo* by Italian sculptor Gaetano Russo at Columbus Circle. Not to be outdone by the Italians, the Spanish also claimed Columbus as their own and placed a statue of him by Spaniard Jerónimo Suñol on the Mall. Celebrating the liberation of Latin America, their countrymen placed Cuban *José Martí,* Bolivian *Simon Bolívar,* and Argentinean *José de San Martín* at the head of the Avenue of the Americas. The Danish, who gave us the beloved storyteller *Hans Christian Andersen,* also donated the statue of his acquaintance and fellow countryman sculptor *Albert Bertel Thorvaldsen.* Displayed collectively, this public art helped to reinforce the uniqueness of America's multicultural complexion and ameliorate social tensions.

Above: Monuments such as William Tecumseh Sherman *taught Park visitors about American history. Left: A bust of Alexander von Humboldt, the most famous intellectual of the nineteenth century, greeted visitors at the main entrance to Central Park. The statue, placed in 1869 by German Americans wishing to honor their revered countryman, contributed to creating a new American institution that acknowledged the cultural diversity of the nation.*

When traveling north through Scholars' Gate, both pedestrians and riders arrive shortly at the sunken transverse road that crosses under the Park at 65th Street. We barely notice this roadway, as it is usually hidden behind a screen of plantings. Furthermore, today's visitors tend to take these types of thoroughfares for granted, resembling as they do the typical over- and underpasses of our modern highway system. In fact, this obscured roadway represents the most important technological innovation of the Olmsted/Vaux plan.

In the competition for the Park's design, the commissioners stipulated that "four or more crossings from east to west must be made between Fifty-ninth and One Hundred and Sixth Street." All of the other entries placed these

required roads within the Park, thereby creating at least eight potentially disruptive traffic intersections. Olmsted and Vaux, however, were at the cutting edge of technology. Ten years before the first underground transportation experiment, they designed a "sub way" that sunk the transverse roads below the level of the Park. Olmsted and Vaux cited the "street that passes through the Regent's Park of London, at the Zoological Gardens" as an earlier example of a pedestrian path running beneath a roadway.[18] In doing so they not only anticipated the bi-level system on which the city's twentieth-century subway system was founded, but also took the first step toward our modern highway system. Both below and inside the Park, the roads were state-of-the-art constructions, making a trip to the Park in the early days far more pleasant than travel on the rutted and muddy streets of the lower city.

Above: The four sunken transverse roads that cross the Park are the most important technological innovations in the Park's design. They are the precursors of our modern highway system.

Left: Vegetation screens out the crosstown traffic below, freeing Park visitors from the noise and bustle of the city.

23

In 1852 a bridge had been proposed to carry pedestrian traffic
over the crowded intersection
of Broadway and Fulton Street
as an attempt to solve the city's
dangerous traffic problem. It
was the first suggestion in New
York of grade separation of
vehicles and pedestrians—but
unlike the innovative subterranean design of Olmsted and
Vaux's transverse roads six years
later, the Broadway bridge forced
pedestrians to climb a steep flight of
stairs. When it was finally erected in
1866, the bridge was a failure, as
New Yorkers were either too lazy or
too hurried to use it. City officials
planned to move it to Central Park,
though it was never installed.

Walking only a few steps further north of the transverse road, pedestrians would arrive at the gleaming white Marble Arch, destroyed in 1941. Using the same bi-level concept as the transverse roads below the Park, the designers separated the pathways within the Park's landscapes through an elaborate system of arches and bridges. The carriage drive brought traffic over the arch while the walkways moved pedestrians below, providing one of the only opportunities in the city to cross a street without interfering with the traffic. The separation of traffic by means of the arches was a truly innovative solution to a dangerous and serious problem. With no concept of order—neither one-way nor two-way traffic—chaos reigned in the busy thoroughfares downtown. As early as 1837, crossing Broadway was considered successful if you got to the other side "with sound bones and a whole skin."[19]

Marble Arch not only represented Yankee ingenuity but also exhibited a uniquely American response to Europe's classical past. Recalling the triumphal arches of antiquity, Olmsted and Vaux created a marble entrance to their formal and processional landscape, the Mall. Unlike its towering Roman counterpart—or one that Vaux had designed with Downing a few years earlier for the Mall in Washington—the Central Park archway was well camouflaged. Built into a slope and barely visible from the carriage drive, it was placed off-center from the Mall so it would not intrude into the most important sight line—the view up the Mall to the Ramble and Vista Rock in the distance. Ironically, this subtle subversion was named after Marble Arch, the famous triumphal entrance placed in London's Hyde Park in 1851.

Top and bottom: The Marble Arch, the theatrical entranceway to the Mall, featured a double staircase to a subterranean seating alcove and drinking fountain. It was the most complex archway in the Park, and was demolished in 1941 to better accommodate automobile traffic on the drive above.

As a result of healthful water, the city experienced a huge population explosion, thus necessitating the expansion of the reservoir system. After much delibera-tion, officials chose to place the new billion-gallon reservoir—the Park's current reservoir —directly north of the first one, from 86th Street to 96th Street.

The interior of Marble Arch featured a drinking fountain of cool, refreshing Croton water, a technological wonder that awed and refreshed Park visitors, who did not take a drink of pure, cold water for granted. [20] The completion of the Croton water system, which brought pure water to a disease-infested New York City in 1842, was like the eighth wonder of the world. In the nineteenth century, clean water was a preoccupation for all growing cities as cholera, a water-borne disease, caused the death of many newborn infants and young children. Within a few years of each other New York, Boston, and Philadelphia developed systems to provide disease-free water to its residents. The Croton water system was a miraculous boon to public health and a major source of civic pride, symbolizing "the wealth, the enterprise, the science and the sagacity of the people of New York."[21]

The recommendation to develop a "central park" in the rocky swampland surrounding the two existing reservoirs was first proposed in 1851 by Nicholas Dean, president of the Croton Aqueduct Board and Henry Shaw, an uptown alderman. Many New Yorkers considered the advanced technology of the reservoirs "the jewels of the park."

*Bronze-and-granite drinking foun-
tains brought iced water to grateful
and surprised Park visitors, unaccus-
tomed to such modern amenities.
Pure Croton water was pumped over
blocks of ice that were taken from
the Park's water bodies in the winter, stored, and placed below the
drinking fountain in deep pits.*

*The crystal-clear waters of the reser-
voirs provided the Park with a
source for its lakes, streams, and
fountains such as the ones that
graced the northern end of the Mall.
They were demolished about 1923
when the Bandshell was constructed.*

*Twenty-five years before the Park
was built, the receiving reservoir
was part of a new system that
brought clean water to New York
City from the dammed-up Croton
River thirty-eight miles to the north.
Drained in 1931, today it is the site
of the Great Lawn.*

THE MALL, A DEMOCRATIC EXPERIENCE

The three separate pathways that entered the Park might inadvertently have mirrored a stratified society, but the Mall and Bethesda Terrace put everyone on equal footing. More than any other Park landscape, the Mall symbolizes Vaux's democratic "ideas into trees and dirt"—Central Park's daring and successful experiment to integrate public space.[22] Comparable to famous European promenades such as the Piazza San Marco in Venice or the Champs-

Élysées in Paris, it was the social arena in which "to see and be seen," although—unlike those European examples—the American promenade brought together a much more diverse and multicultural population.

The emergence of a market economy and urban culture created an incentive for public promenading in the early 1850s. The concept did not seem to be a radical idea by 1858, and many entrants in the design competition

The Mall in 1905.

included a formal promenade in their plans. But, as we have seen, pleasant social interaction of all classes in public places was frightful and infrequent. Olmsted himself described the anxiety, suspicion, and mistrust that determined his body language in public:

> to merely avoid collision with those we meet and pass upon the sidewalks, we have constantly to watch, to foresee, and to guard against their movements. This involves a consideration of their intentions, calculations of their strength and weaknesses.[23]

These codes of behavior, in turn, influenced the design of the few public walks that preceded Central Park, featuring circular paths so that people could avoid the taboo of a direct confrontational stare.[24] It was fine to promenade up and down Main Street in small-town America, where there was a homogeneous population, but in heterogeneous cities people wanted to circumvent the unknown.

The landscape sequence of the Mall and Bethesda Terrace is the only straight line in Central Park.[25] The designers stated in their original plan that they were "averse on general principles to a symmetrical arrangement of trees,"

Above: In the nineteenth century every Main Street and college campus across the country was lined with an allée of graceful American elms. In the 1930s Dutch elm disease, a fungus that arrived from Holland, began to devastate most of the American species. Today the 150 elms on the Mall and the two and a half miles of elms along Fifth Avenue are the two largest stands of American elms on the North American continent.

Left: The Mall, a formal promenade, was designed to be the only straight line in Central Park.

Right: When the Park was under construction, there was a loud demand from an impatient public for large trees. Elms were chosen for their beautiful branching patterns, and also because it was thought that very large trees could be transplanted. In November 1858, the New York Times *reported that the contractor would be paid thirty dollars apiece for all trees that lived at least three years, "and nothing for the failures." The first plantings all died that first year. The second planting of elms grew to maturity by the 1890s. Unfortunately, their mature roots could not penetrate the deep, hard clay soil in which they were planted, and they began to die by the turn of the century. Today's elms were planted about 1920.*

Left: Olmsted's passion for the tropical landscapes he saw in Panama gave him the spiritual rapture of a religious experience. Using plantings that would survive in New York's temperate zone, Olmsted and his horticulture expert Ignaz Pilat wanted to create the impression of that lush landscape on the shoreline of the Ramble and the island in the Lake.

preferring romantic, curvilinear paths that meandered through the changing topography. Nonetheless, they felt that such a formal design was appropriate for landscapes that catered to the social needs of a metropolitan park. Furthermore, the walk north up the Mall rewarded each promenader with the single most important view in the Park—the Ramble and the tower atop Vista Rock (Belvedere Castle after its construction in 1869).

Landscape architects use trees and shrubs to create "rooms" in the same way that architects use bricks and lumber. So it is no coincidence that the quadruple row of American elms on the Mall suggests the interior of a Gothic cathedral. In fact, in 1858 when the Mall was under construction, the *New York Times* referred to the Mall as "the Cathedral Walk."[26] The quarter-mile procession of stately trees resembles columns aligning a nave and side aisles. Fifty feet overhead, the trees' interlocking branches suggest the graceful arabesque forms of Gothic ribbed vaulting, while the golden sunlight flickering on the leaves glows like stained-glass windows. The sculptures that line the walk echo private chapels dedicated to venerated literary figures. On spring and summer afternoons visitors were customarily drawn northward by the sound of music, as the space opens up into the "choir loft," known informally as "the concert ground." Descending into the darkened Terrace arcade, adorned with Gothic and Romanesque carvings and colorfully glazed ceiling tiles, they arrive at the heart of the Park—the dazzling, open-air apse of the Terrace. Crowning the central high altar—the Biblical Pool of Bethesda—was the blessed messenger angel of God.[27]

It is not surprising to speak metaphorically of ecclesiastical structure and religious symbolism at the heart of Central Park. The Park was created to be a moral landscape, and religion was at the heart of the most esteemed and cherished of all values. During the early to mid-nineteenth century, however, traditional systems of belief were being confronted with serious challenges. At this time there was a prodigious influx of new scientific information and investigation, culminating in the radical theories of Englishmen Charles Lyell and Charles Darwin. Charles Lyell's profoundly important work on geology, *Principles of Geology,*

published in 1830–33, introduced to modern thought the concept of deep time and shattered the popular notion that the earth was formed in Biblical time only 5,000 years earlier. In 1859 Charles Darwin's theory of natural selection in his *On the Origin of the Species* would deal the most crushing blow of all to the belief in a God-centered universe of structure and order, forcing Protestant Americans to redefine the ways they worshipped God.

Americans, who took great pride in the natural wonders of their continent, found God everywhere in nature. Barbara Novak in her masterful work, *Nature and Culture,* describes this new nature-centered religion: "In the early nineteenth century in America, nature couldn't do without God, and God apparently couldn't do without nature. Ideas of God's nature and of God in nature became hopelessly entangled. If nature was God's Holy Book, it was God."[28]

These scientists as well as many nature-centered theologians, writers, and religious thinkers heavily influenced the designers of the Park, who also considered nature their spiritual source. Frederick Law Olmsted worshipped at the altar of nature, and his writings are infused with a religious reverence. While traveling through the straits of Panama in 1863, for example, his encounter with tropical vegetation jolted him with the rapture and urgency of a spiritual awakening: "I am thoroughly enchanted with the trees and vines. But cane and palms are not trees or vines or shrubs or herbs. They are Gloria in Excelsis with lots of exclamation points thrown in any where, in the grand choral liturgy."[29]

Olmsted's reverence for "the profound sense of the Creator's bountifulness"[30] was most evident in the Park's horticultural plans and designs, done in collaboration with his superintendent of plantings, Ignaz Pilat. Their most important horticultural creation was the Ramble, an "American garden," on the direct axis of the Mall.

BETHESDA TERRACE

Olmsted's partner, architect Calvert Vaux, realized his reverence for the divinity of nature at Bethesda Terrace, the Park's greatest architectural space. Situated between the Mall and the Ramble, the Terrace and fountain adjacent to the Lake were intended to combine symbolically all the political and cultural aspirations of the Park and its creators. This artistic masterpiece-within-the-masterpiece of Central Park merits a chapter of its own.

Bethesda Terrace in 1905.

Bethesda Terrace is the defining feature

of Central Park, contributing greatly to

its status as the most important work of

nineteenth-century American art. In the

previous chapter, we saw how each feature

along our route—from the gate at 60th Street

to the elms along the Mall—represented

a significant social, political, artistic,

or technological aspect of mid-nineteenth-

century culture. At the Terrace, Calvert

Vaux merged the naturalistic landscape

with an ambitious architectural program,

the vision and scope of which was never

again matched in any other public park.

Vaux's architectural masterpiece, conceived and created before, during, and after the Civil War, reflects a pivotal moment in American history and places Central Park at the fulcrum of the period's art and culture. Just before Central Park consumed the life of Calvert Vaux, he wrote in the introduction to his book *Villas and Cottages* that he wanted a new architecture that "show[ed] it to be a genuine American invention."[1] At Bethesda Terrace he realized that vision in collaboration with his talented and bohemian colleague Jacob Wrey Mould.

Bethesda Terrace has been called "the heart of the Park" since 1864. In 1863 Calvert Vaux proposed an elaborate sculptural program for Bethesda Terrace that included many freestanding bronze sculptures. The fountain is the only one that was ever completed.

Bethesda Terrace connects a formal architectural space with the pastoral Lake and the picturesque woodlands of the Ramble. Cherry Hill plaza and fountain can be seen above the Terrace esplanade.

English-born architect and designer Jacob Wrey Mould was a close colleague and collaborator of Calvert Vaux. Mould studied architecture and ornamentation in England with Owen Jones, and is credited with assisting him on the decoration for London's highly ornate Crystal Palace of 1851 and for the "Mooresque-Turkish divan" for Buckingham Palace. He is said to have spent time in Spain at the Alhambra, the medieval Moorish architectural complex, in order to work on the drawings for the 1848 second volume of Jones's book on the subject—the often-cited source for the ornamental carvings of Bethesda Terrace. Mould has also been cited as an illustrator for Jones's books: Gray's *Elegy* (1846), the *Book of Common Prayer* (1849), and *The Grammar of Ornament* (1856). [2]

When Mould immigrated to America in 1853, he designed the All Souls Unitarian Church on 20th Street and Fourth Avenue. Called the "Church of the Holy Zebra" because of its striped stone exterior, the Italian Gothic structure was a radical addition to the otherwise staid architecture of New York City. Vaux must have invited the talented designer to join the Park staff when he began the initial design work for the Terrace in late 1858. [3]

In the Greensward plan, a drawing by Mould depicts Calvert Vaux's vision for a bi-level arcade featuring a series of Romanesque arches in combination with figurative sculptures (see page 97). It was not intended, however, for the "Italian" terrace at the end of the Mall, but rather for the Garden Arcade proposed at Fifth Avenue and Seventy-fourth Street—now Conservatory Water. The abrupt change in the topography from the avenue to the lower ground within the Park ensured a natural viewing platform for the decorative flower beds and main fountain below. The designers explained that their lakeside terrace—the one that eventually became Bethesda Terrace—was "not absolutely necessary," and roughly sketched out only a single staircase with balustrades that opened onto an esplanade and a round basin for the fountain. Once the Park was under construction, however, changes gradually took place at both sites. By 1862 the original plans for the Garden Arcade and the Italian Terrace were conflated into one grand thematic conception, featuring the bi-level arcade of Romanesque arches, life-size bronze and marble sculptures, and the main central fountain that became Bethesda Terrace.

Jacob Wrey Mould, the bohemian architect and designer of the Terrace carvings, shown beside the spring pier.

Vaux's comprehensive sculptural program for Bethesda Terrace, published in January 1863, called for many bronze and marble allegorical figures that were never created.[4] At the head of the flight of steps as one enters from the Mall, Vaux dedicated the two piers to "Day" and "Night." In keeping with that theme, the proposed bronze sculptures along the south side of the 72nd Street cross-drive were meant to represent "Sunlight," "Moonlight," "Starlight," and "Twilight." Directly across the drive, Vaux called for bronze representations of the four ages of man: "Childhood," "Youth," "Maturity," and "Old Age."

The ramps, balustrades, and piers leading down to the lower Terrace—which contain the most famous of the executed carvings—represent the four seasons, a theme often equated with the ages of man. From east to west "Spring," "Summer," "Autumn," and "Winter" are depicted. The four flat piers at the landings were also intended to hold statues for each season, and the four empty shields on these piers were intended to hold "illustrative quotations from the poets." The lateral piers on the extreme eastern and western wings of the Terrace were intended to display four geographic elements, "The Mountain," "The Valley," "The River," and "The Lake." On the lower terrace and directly facing each staircase Vaux envisioned two multi-figured groups, one representing "Science" and the other representing "Art."

Vaux proposed to place the most elaborate sculptural group on the Terrace below the large glass panel on the arcade ceiling, so that "a tempered light [would be] shed directly over [it] and appear to emanate from it." Representing "Nature," the sculpture was to be composed of four separate marble figures—Flora, Pomona, Sylva, and Ceres—displayed in niches or shallow recesses and adorned with vases containing sculptures of their respective botanical equivalents: flowers, fruit, forest leaves, and grasses.

The fountain at the heart of the Terrace, which Vaux called "the centre of the centre," was intended to encapsulate his theme: it "should suggest both earnestly and playfully the idea of that central spirit of 'Love' that is for ever active, and for ever bringing nature, science, art, summer and winter, youth and age, day and night, into harmonious accord."[5]

Vaux and the commissioners knew that public funds would be inadequate to complete the bronze sculptures for the Terrace and hoped that private citizens would commission eminent artists to fill the vacant pedestals. Skeptical of finding competent American sculptors in the mid-nineteenth century, art critic Clarence Cook stated, "If one statue is found fit to be placed upon the Terrace in a generation, we shall think we are getting on very well indeed."

Vaux's Influences

Interpretations of the interconnectedness of all life and its place within the cycles of the universe have been man's preoccupation from prehistory to the scientific age in the nineteenth century. Vaux's encyclopedic vision belongs to that long tradition and, though he never cited a source for his "earnest general idea," he was certainly familiar with the work of three important nineteenth-century figures whose criticism, natural philosophy, and art focused on these cycles: John Ruskin, Alexander von Humboldt, and Thomas Cole.

JOHN RUSKIN

In the world of art, architecture, and aesthetics, no one was more influential or widely read in mid-century England and America than British artist and critic John Ruskin. A deeply religious man, Ruskin recognized God's presence in the natural world as well as in the art of man. As a reaction to the Industrial Revolution's mass-produced goods and materials, the writer celebrated the work of medieval craftsmen, particularly in the churches of Venice and northern Italy, who designed *and* carved their stonework themselves.

Through Ruskin's eyes, Vaux and Mould looked to such architectural models and standards of craftsmanship for their aesthetic guidance and artistic sensibility. Ruskin's two most acclaimed books on architecture, *The Seven Lamps of Architecture* (1849) and *The Stones of Venice* (1853), were keystones of mid-Victorian architectural theory in England and America, and they would have been important to Vaux and Mould's architectural education.

We have already compared the design of the Mall and the Terrace to the plan of a Gothic cathedral. So too the design and subject matter of Vaux's Terrace program echoed the designs and programs of medieval churches so admired by Ruskin. The sculptural programs on the portals of the Byzantine basilica of San Marco in Venice and of the Gothic cathedrals of Notre-Dame in Paris and Chartres functioned like a Bible to be "read" by worshipers as they entered the church. Biblical stories, scenes from the life of Christ, saints, apostles, and patriarchs covered the doors, tympana, and jambs of the portals. Frequently, carvings would also include subjects such as the signs of the zodiac, seasonal labors, personifications of the liberal arts, mythical beings, and the flora and fauna of the natural world. Together, the sculptures represented a comprehensive and unified understanding of the cosmos according to medieval thought. This type of encyclopedic program was the foundation for Vaux's Terrace, which would have been understood by both cultivated visitors and those who lacked a formal education.

ALEXANDER VON HUMBOLDT

Just as the medieval cathedral displayed God's view of the cosmos, so too did Vaux's Terrace reflect "the harmonious accord pervading the universe" as theorized by German natural philosopher and scientist Alexander von Humboldt. Most educated individuals in the nineteenth century, including Calvert Vaux, would have been familiar with Humboldt and his five-volume life work *Kosmos,* published beginning in 1845 and translated into English in 1850, perhaps the most widely read science book ever published.[6] Humboldt constructed a rational system of the universe that united new scientific developments with traditionally held beliefs.[7] "Nature is a unity in diversity of phenomena;

a harmony, blending together all created things, however dissimilar in form and attributes; one great whole animated by the breath of life."[8] *Cosmos* (as it is known in English) attempted to explain the interconnection among the diverse natural cycles in astronomy, geology, geography, meteorology, botany, and zoology—disciplines that were being redefined in the late eighteenth and early nineteenth centuries. These endeavors would have been allegorized by the "Science" grouping at the foot of one staircase. Furthermore, Humboldt recognized art as the most powerful expression that man had constructed in his attempt to understand nature. He had a deep appreciation for landscape painting in particular, as well as poetry and the Romantic style of English parks that brought urban man in touch with the natural world, to be represented on the Terrace by personifications of "Art." Therefore, it is not surprising that Calvert Vaux would illustrate Humboldt's comprehensive system of natural philosophy as the centerpiece of a park that was intended to be the equivalent of contemporary landscape painting and an allegorical microcosm of *Cosmos*.

THOMAS COLE

Calvert Vaux, whose brother-in-law was Hudson River School painter Jervis McEntee, was undoubtedly familiar with the allegorical painting cycles done by contemporary artists such as Asher B. Durand and Jasper Cropsey. But perhaps the most far-reaching influence on Vaux would have been *The Voyage of Life* series (1839–42) done by the school's founder, English-born painter Thomas Cole. Cole's famous cycle related to the four stages of a man's life, depicting *Childhood, Youth, Manhood, Old Age,* in four canvases. [9] The paintings parallel a stage of life with the appropriate season of the year, the time of day, and meteorological conditions. Cole's interpretation of this universal theme was so popular that engravings of this work were "almost as often found in American homes between 1850 and 1875 as had been engravings of George Washington in an earlier generation."[10] The accessibility and popularity of the theme would have appealed to both the designers and the commissioners, concerned as they were with engaging and enlightening the widest possible democratic audience.

Bronze statues representing the four ages of man, a popular theme in nineteenth-century art and literature, were intended for Bethesda Terrace. The Voyage of Life, Childhood (1839) by Thomas Cole is one of four in the artist's series of paintings on the subject. In Cole's paintings, as in the carvings on the stairways, each stage of life is equated to a season of the year and often a time of day as well. This work depicts childhood, spring, and sunrise.

Carvings of seasonal flora and
fauna are represented on the four
balustrades of the main staircase
of the Terrace. The flat pier at the
top of the landing was intended to
feature a bronze personification
of spring.

This page: The autumn pier depicts the bounty of the season: sensuously carved
grapes and tendrils are paired with the head of a stag, a prize for a fall hunter.
Opposite, top row: A nest of eggs and hatchlings is represented on the spring pier;
the bees and their honeycomb symbolize the busy work of summer.
Opposite, bottom row: A brace of quail is a sign of fall; the winter pier depicts
the hatchlings as mature birds.

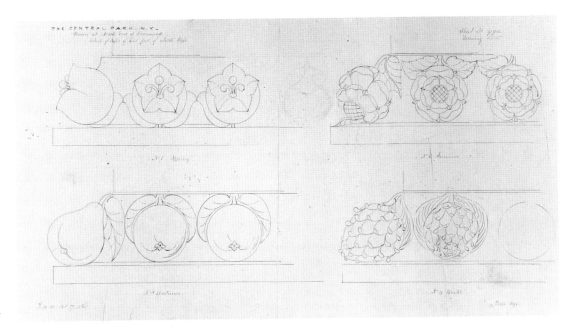

This drawing featuring apple blossoms (spring), apples (autumn), roses (summer), and pinecones (winter) is the only surviving drawing by Mould of seasonal details.

The carved apples surrounding the top of the autumn pier.

Above the viewing platform on the 72nd Street cross-drive Vaux had suggested bronze representations of the four ages of man—"Childhood," "Youth," "Manhood," and "Old Age"—that would relate directly to the four seasons below them.[11]

The carvings of the four seasons reflect the passion for botany in the eighteenth and nineteenth centuries, when it was common to decorate the home with seasonal imagery. In the late eighteenth century, for example, the theme appears in the English manor house at Stowe, a site that would have been known to Vaux and Mould. The grand staircase was adorned with paintings of the four seasons, while statues of *Flora*, *Pomona*, and *Ceres*—three of the four sculptural allegories intended for the "Nature" grouping under the Bethesda arcade—were placed above the center pavilion.[12]

The nineteenth century was also the age of passionate amateur naturalists and their preoccupation with collecting and classifying specimens of the natural world. Nearly every middle-class Victorian home gathered and displayed mosses, ferns, and tiny plants in a popular glass "Wardian case" that today we would call a terrarium. Artists, scientists, and the general public were tireless students of botanic observation, filling sketchbook after sketchbook with minute details of flowers, leaves, fruit, and grasses. In fact, botanical sketching, an activity that actually required a permit, was one of the most popular Park pastimes.

Jacob Wrey Mould was no exception. The sculptures on the Terrace represent a virtual encyclopedia of botanical specimens in each season, hardly a detail repeated, and these panels and their companion balustrades and piers on the lower Terrace are Mould's finest work. This fascination with nature observation is particularly evident in the

Above: A carving of a pair of charming nineteenth-century ice-skates on the winter balustrade is the only man-made object depicted among the natural subjects.

Right: Emma Stebbins, the sculptor of the Bethesda Fountain, created this figure of "Autumn" and three other plaster models of the four seasons for Bethesda Terrace in an attempt to secure the prestigious commission.

Each season was depicted with the most representative flora and fauna, which delight us even today. The trillium and dogwood are familiar signs of spring. Plump strawberries, raspberries, and roses capture summer's bounty. Corn and pears represent autumn, and delicate ferns, ivy, thorns, and gnarled and leafless branches remind us of the tenacity and beauty of nature even during the sparse winter season.

marvelous details on the four balustrades, carved to represent a garden trellis. The faithfully rendered fruit, flowers, plants, and animals on both the panels and the four balustrades reveal Mould's close attention to "truth in nature," one of the most important principles espoused by Ruskin, who regarded drawing directly from nature as the highest form of artistic expression. The drawings in stone that Mould created for the Terrace are a testament to his devotion to Ruskin's aesthetic philosophy. Sensuous details such as the grapes and tendrils below the stag on the autumn pier or a group of brilliantly tactile and playful icicles—one of the most delightful surprises on the western side of the winter pier—display a breathtaking sensitivity on the part of both Mould and the excellent carvers who brought his two-dimensional drawings to life. These botanical illustrations

are pure pleasure, both for their appreciation of nature's diversity and for man's ability to interpret and reproduce it.

A discreet carving on the rear of the winter balustrade serves as a chilling reminder that Bethesda Terrace was conceived and created during the winter of our nation's discontent. A rectangle featuring a ribbonlike cross and five five-pointed stars can be found among the expected seasonal carvings of bare branches and dried seedpods. This enigmatic carving might allude to the military insignia of a Union soldier, a battle flag, or currency. Whatever its specific identity, it is almost certainly a reference to the war that was raging between the North and South. Whether created by Vaux, Mould, or an independent-minded carver, it suggests some form of patriotic sentiment that was foremost in the hearts and minds of Americans.[13]

Despite the designers' desire to suspend references to worldly affairs in the refuge of Central Park, important symbolic allusions to local, state, and national preoccupations were represented on the Terrace. Vaux's program culminated in the sculptures of the eastern and western wings of the Terrace, which symbolized four geographic elements: "The Mountain," "The Valley," and "The River" are features not represented in Central Park; only "The Lake" had any internal reference, albeit a man-made one. Nonetheless, these four geographic features were included in almost every work of American nineteenth-century landscape art. Whether in painted form or sculpted allegory, they glorify the nation's most treasured asset—the land itself.

When the war was at its height, the commissioners took up valuable space in the annual report for the year 1864 to

Above: A discreet carving hidden on the back of the winter balustrade refers to the political turmoil of the Civil War years, which coincided with the construction of the Terrace.

Above: In the years before the Civil War, the flags framing the Terrace represented New York State and New York City. The American flag, flying between them from the distant Vista Rock, was positioned to celebrate Central Park as the pride of national, state, and city government.

Opposite: Bethesda Terrace is the most elaborate example of civic architecture in mid-nineteenth-century America.

boast about the primacy of the American landscape and to decree that Central Park—New York's "chief work"—honors these national treasures:

> [B]y general consent naturalists accord to our own continent marked superiority of vegetable life. Its trees are peculiarly numerous and majestic, its fields, luxuriant and prolific, its flowers brilliant and varied. It seems appropriate then, that this city should in its chief work endeavor to mark and emphasize this characteristic of the country, from every river, plain, and mountain side, of whose broad latitudes are derived the bounteous supports of its present growth, and the well founded promises of its future greatness.[14]

The Park in general and the Terrace specifically not only were reflections of national pride but also visible symbols of New York's affluence and its leadership in America's economic and cultural life. When Vaux first developed the program for the Terrace in 1859 or 1860, the commissioners were preoccupied with financial constraints and made no mention of an elaborate sculptural program.[15] After war broke out in 1861, however, the additional expense for the Terrace became politically justified and financially possible. New York City experienced an enormous economic surge after the attack on Fort Sumter; its industrial production almost surpassed that of the entire Confederacy.[16] The Park, in the eyes of many, became a symbolic centerpiece of Northern civilization, and the Terrace evolved into the centerpiece of the Park.

Vaux placed the flags of New York City and New York State as the essential framing device for his most important work of art—a constant reminder of the centrality of Central Park in feelings of civic pride. Prior to the war, the natural scenery of the Ramble and Vista Rock was described by the designers as the most important view from the Mall and Terrace. By 1863, however, Vaux shifted the "culminating point of interest" to be the stars and stripes of the American flag, centrally positioned over the Terrace from the top of Vista Rock, serving to unify the hopes and prayers for the endurance of the nation.[17]

The Terrace was not only the heart of Central Park, it was also dear to the heart and soul of Calvert Vaux. It was the most important part of the Park to him, and by his own admission the Terrace was "the only thing that gives me much encouragement that I have in me the germ of an architect."[18] Vaux wanted visitors to be drawn through the simple gates at the entrance to the Park into the naturalistic environment, conceived as a carefully orchestrated experience. As he stated, "Nature first, and 2nd & 3rd, Architecture after a while."[19] With no natural feature such as a mountain for the focal point of the vista, Olmsted and Vaux chose to create an architectural structure that was set into the landscape. The formality of the elm allée prepared the visitor for the formality of the Terrace, the most innovative and elaborate work of civic architecture created in America.

In the spring of 1863, while the Terrace was under construction and the War between the States was underway, a war between the gates raged in Central Park. The battle over the design of the gates represented a major threat to the importance of Bethesda Terrace and the symbolic role it played in the Park. It would require Olmsted and Vaux to defend their urban retreat against the contrary vision of architect Richard Morris Hunt, who wanted to integrate Central Park with the city in a celebration of civic grandeur.

In 1855, Vermont-born Hunt had recently returned to New York after a ten-year residence in Paris, where he had been the first American to study architecture at the prestigious and influential École des Beaux-Arts. To Olmsted and Vaux, Hunt's vision—grandiose classical monuments at the end of long urban vistas, such as the Arc de Triomphe and the Champs-Élysées— represented French imperialism over American republican ideals. Mocking Olmsted and Vaux's rural design for Central Park Hunt exclaimed, "How absurd, then, it is to cheat ourselves into the belief this is

always to be a sylvan retreat fit for shepherds and their flock."[20] And Hunt also had an ace up his sleeve: Commissioner Charles H. Russell, his wealthy and powerful brother-in-law, who prodded the other board members to give support to Hunt's monumental gateway project.[21] With so much of his professional integrity and self-esteem at stake in the Terrace, it was, therefore, a devastating blow to Calvert Vaux when the commissioners voted to adopt Hunt's gates, declaring, "[T]he Park is to be enjoyed not only on reaching particular centres or places, but at the very entrance, and at each succeeding step."[22] This slap in the face caused Vaux to quit and convinced Olmsted, who was working in California in May 1863, to resign as well, leaving the completion of Vaux's beloved Terrace in the hands of his colleague "that strange genius, Wrey Mould."[23]

Once Hunt's designs were adopted, however, the board vacillated again, much to Commissioner Russell's exasperation. It issued a statement in the 1864 *Annual Report* supporting natural elements as the only suitable subject for art in a democratic Park, negating Hunt's Beaux-Arts conception and, once again, embracing Vaux's natural subjects on the Terrace.

> [V]egetation should hold the first place of distinction; it is the work of nature, invulnerable to criticism, accepted by all, as well the cultivated as the ignorant. . . . Neither variety in design nor poverty in detail are wanting in the school in which nature is the exemplar; architecture and all the kindred arts that are brought into use on the Park, rejecting all symbolisms of classic and pagan mythology as things of a past civilization, and leaving out the petrified emblems of exploded faiths, should be submissive to the predominance of nature and illustrate the purer faith of the age. [24]

The board's important pronouncement, though tied to no specific project, was certainly its unofficial rejection of Hunt's gates, which included many Greek and Roman deities. The commissioners once again embraced the natural world that was reflected in the program by Vaux and the carvings by Mould.

Richard Morris Hunt's design for the Scholars' Gate was adopted by the board of commissioners in 1863 over the objections of architect Calvert Vaux, who subsequently resigned his position along with his partner, Frederick Law Olmsted. Hunt's gates featured a four-hundred-foot-wide square plaza with a central fountain and a split-level, semicircular terrace featuring a fifty-foot classical column bearing the arms of New York City. The column, held by a Native American and a mariner, stood atop a rectangular basin, which depicted the figure of Henry Hudson on the prow of an antique ship and between the personifications of the Hudson and East Rivers. Heading down to the Pond, a double cascade-lined flight of stairs descended into a basin with a jet spray and a grotto featuring Neptune and his chariot. The plans were dropped by 1865.

The four main carvings at the northern end of the Mall, intended by Vaux to represent the times of day, seem quite different from the flora and fauna found on the ramps and staircases across the drive. The rooster on the east pier, the universal avian symbol of "Day," and its counterpart, the owl on the west, a symbol of "Night," are thematically similar. The other four scenes also reflect Vaux's initial conception but are less obvious to modern viewers, as they reflect cultural symbols more familiar to nineteenth-century America. With the exception of *Little Peachblossom,* an 1873 Christian children's guide to the Park, these carvings have never been discussed either in nineteenth-century or present-day literature, leaving us the task of shedding some light on these important works for the first time.[25]

The easternmost panel on the "Day" pier depicts the rising sun and its floral equivalent, the sunflower. For a representation of this daily phenomenon, Mould carved out a deep space and lined it with the familiar radiating lines that even young children draw to portray the light from the sun. In the early morning this "void" is filled with the sun's direct rays. Brilliantly and simply, Mould created a sculpture that literally captures the morning light.

Equating the sun with God had been a metaphor common to almost every religion in every culture from ancient Egypt and Greece to nineteenth-century America. Ruskin equated light with God in his widely read guide to art and aesthetics, *Modern Painters.*[26] Contemporary American landscape painters, wanting to express the interrelationship of God and nature, chose light as the subject of the works themselves. Frederick Church, for example, often titled his paintings according to the time of day: for example, *Morning* (1848), *Twilight, "Short Arbiter Twixt Day and Night"* (1850), and *Morning in the Tropics* (1856). Whether

the artists depicted the peaks of the Hudson Valley, the lakes of New England, or the ruins of Italy and Jerusalem, they preferred to capture the mystical hours at sunrise, twilight, or sunset, which best expressed God as light. In his written description of the project, Vaux too chose those poetic hours: "Sunlight," represented by the rising sun, "Moonlight," "Starlight," and "Twilight." Clearly, he was trying to represent the aesthetic and spiritual times of day, according to the painter or poet.

The inner side of the "Day" pier depicts an agricultural scene. Bundled sheaves of wheat are shown alongside a humble thatch-roofed farmhouse. A scythe, a shovel, and a rake—now severely weathered— represent man's physical dependence on the natural world through his daily work. This scene resembles the "July" or "August" illustrations of reaping from a medieval Book of Hours or its more popular nineteenth-century American equivalents. As seen in respect to the Park's gates, the American work ethic and the Protestant beliefs on which those values were founded are as bound together as those stalks of grain in the field.[27]

Yet the bundles of wheat may also have had a more chauvinistic meaning for New Yorkers. In 1860 and 1861, the wheat crop in Europe and Britain failed, while America produced the most abundant harvests in years.[28] America's bounty was exported to Europe on ships sent forth from New York Harbor, resulting in an enormous flood of capital and power to a metropolis that was already booming from the economic benefits of the Civil War. Furthermore, wheat symbolized the economy of the Union in the same way that cotton represented the Confederacy. At the time that these panels were carved, the nation had just been embroiled in an internal conflict that was the direct outcome of two divergent economic systems—one based on a paid labor

The spring ramp.

force, the other on the institution of slavery. The wheat farm thus received a place of honor at the entrance to the Terrace, a reminder to Park visitors of America's bountiful landscapes, the moral superiority of the North, and the civic pride and wealth of New York—all the direct result of our earthly abundance.[29]

The companion pier, "Night," located on the western side of the steps, also represents work to be done. After the physical labor of day, one's spiritual work began—the reading and interpreting of the Holy Word, here represented by an open Bible, which was read daily by most nineteenth-century Americans. Protestant sects assigned to each believer the responsibility for his or her own truths, and salvation rested on reading and reflecting on Scripture. The hourglass, now a badly damaged fragment, reminded practical and pious Americans that the time to prepare for one's eternal life with God was at hand. This was a subtle message telling visitors to commune with God through His presence in nature, often referred to as "God's Second Holy Book."[30] The Bible, the lamp, and the hourglass clearly rest on a small pulpit, an allusion to the natural world as "God's pulpit."

For the designers of the Terrace, the very prominent Arabian lamp combined with the book could have been a veiled reference to their "Bible," Ruskin's *The Seven*

Lamps of Architecture. Art critic Clarence Cook, Vaux's close friend, was a devout Ruskin protégé and even referred to him as "'the mystic lamp-lighter' whose seven lamps had done so much to illuminate architectural criticism [and] to center it on the love of nature and the love of God."[31] In his most important book, Ruskin defines the guiding principles or "lamps" of architecture with these words of God: "The Law is Light, Thy Word is a lamp unto my feet."[32] There is no question that Mould and Vaux, trained by the light of Ruskin's "lamps," would have considered the carvings and proposed sculptures as a visual text for the teaching of God in nature, just like those works on the facades of medieval cathedrals that Ruskin so revered.

In comparison to the traditional "Night" owl and bat facing the Mall, the Halloween scene is both familiar and surprising. It is hard to believe that these holiday symbols, which seem so commercial in our contemporary culture, could have been carved so long ago. The west-facing illustration is the complement to the east-facing scenes of the rising sun and the Biblical still life. The panel represents both the natural "moonlight" suggested by Vaux and the cultural artifact of the jack-o'-lantern, a protective light carried by the celebrants of ancient, pagan Halloween rituals. A candle placed in a hollowed-out turnip was a longstand-

ing Irish tradition to ward away evil spirits of the dead on All Hallow's Eve. After the wave of Irish immigration of 1848, however, the abundant pumpkin in their adopted country replaced the turnip and thus introduced the tradition so familiar to our culture. Most of the newly arrived immigrants from Ireland were Catholics, but they practiced their Catholicism alongside pre-Christian Celtic peasant traditions.[33] The most important of these rituals was the Celtic New Year, known as *Samhain*—Gaelic for "summer's end" or "the setting of the sun"—which marked the gateway between summer and fall/winter.

The inclusion of this scene on the Terrace could be a symbolic recognition of the Irish population of New York, the city's largest immigrant group, as well as the numerous Irish laborers involved in constructing the Park.[34] The Biblical conventions of the Christian middle and upper classes on the eastern side of the pier can be compared to oral and folk traditions of immigrants on the western side.[35]

Certainly when Vaux suggested that the themes be interpreted "playfully," he would have considered Mould's boundless creative imagination; however, he remained silent forever on his impressions of both the Mall carvings and the centerpiece of his entire creation, the *Angel of the Waters* fountain by Emma Stebbins.

The carvings on the Mall feature representations of "Day" and "Night." From far left to right: the rising sun; the rooster; the wheat farm; the Bible, lamp, and hourglass; the owl and bat; and the Halloween symbols of the witch on a broomstick, the jack-o'-lantern, and the crescent moon.

For the arcade niches Mould created many fanciful and elegant designs that were never completed. Contemporary trompe l'oeil decoration approximates the proposed frescoed or tiled niches.

In his writings and his Terrace work Vaux confirmed Ruskin's insistence on the "close connection between Architecture, Sculpture, and Painting; that Sculpture and Painting . . . this union of the arts [being] necessary for the full development of each."[51] Without painting and sculpture, Ruskin felt that an architect was "nothing better than a frame-maker on a large scale."[52] Sculpture predominated on the exterior of the Terrace, and "painting" took precedence in the underground arcade that connected the Mall with the open-air esplanade and fountain. Mould—whose self-proclaimed remark that he was "Hell on Color"—translated two-dimensional painting into proposed frescoes, elaborately tiled niches, a stained-glass panel, and floor and ceiling tile work. Like a true eclectic, Mould borrowed from many different styles and traditions, particularly that of the flamboyant and colorful medieval Moorish decoration chiefly associated with the Alhambra in Spain and the Venetian Gothic, which conflated European Gothic, Byzantine, and Islamic styles. The results were intended to transform the long and dark cryptlike arcade into a jeweled reception hall whose colorfully tiled surfaces would reflect the Park's natural light.[53]

Sculpture predominated on the exterior of the Terrace and in the arcade in the form of a special marble "Nature" group, featuring Flora, Pomona, Sylva, and Ceres. This elaborate grouping explains the frosted-glass panel still seen in the ceiling. Vaux's inspiration for this multi-figured sculpture can, most likely, be traced to an 1860 gift to Central Park. In 1860 the widow of the late American sculptor Thomas Crawford donated eighty-seven of her husband's plaster casts to establish a museum in the new park (see Chapter 5, page 184). In conjunction with her gift, Richard K. Haight, the owner of Crawford's *Flora*, offered to donate it to the Crawford collection.[54] Vaux, who would have seen this elegant and masterful sculpture at either the Crystal Palace exhibit of 1853 or possibly in Haight's home, would have certainly wanted to incorporate the delicate marble sculpture into his Terrace program, under the protective arcade. The luminosity of the incandescent marble probably caused him to remark on the light, which would "appear to emanate from it." Haight never came through with his donation, and the sculpture is now in the collection of the Newark Museum in Newark, New Jersey.

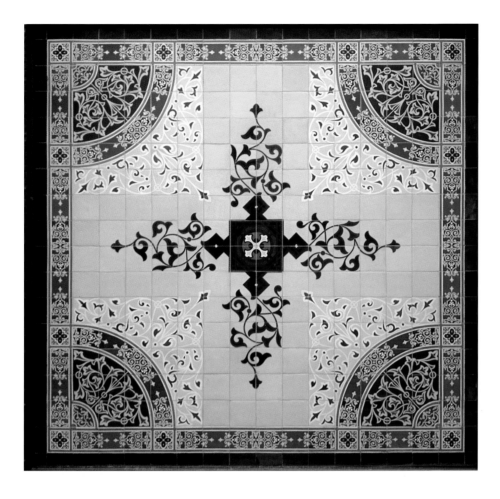

Top: Bethesda Terrace is the only outdoor space, as well as the only ceiling, for which Minton tiles have ever been employed. English architect and designer Owen Jones, a mentor of Jacob Wrey Mould who designed the Terrace tiles, helped Herbert Minton overcome technical difficulties with the new encaustic process in 1828. Jones brought the concept of using Spanish tiles, known as azulejos, back to England after visiting the Alhambra.

Bottom: Drawings of colorful and fanciful tiles proposed for the niches are examples of Mould's decorative plan to bring bright color, gold leaf, and reflected light to the dark tunnel of the Bethesda arcade.

Central Park developed out of close associations: those between landscape painting and landscape design, and those among the individuals responsible, directly or indirectly, for the Park's design and development. In 1849, American artist Asher B. Durand was commissioned to paint *Kindred Spirits* as a gift to the poet William Cullen Bryant for the eulogy he had delivered the year before at the funeral of his close friend, landscape painter Thomas Cole. The painting depicts Cole, sketchbook in hand, standing with Bryant on a rock outcrop over a Catskill mountain ravine. Cole had been the first to paint such wild and untamed scenes of his

adopted country in the mid-1820s, establishing the first true American school of painting, which supplied the pictorial context of Central Park. In Durand's painting, Cole and Bryant symbolize Art as the kindred spirit of Nature, and they represent two men connected to each other through their love of nature—the guiding principle behind the creation of Central Park.

Frederick Law Olmsted and Calvert Vaux were not yet kindred spirits when Durand created the painting, but each man would soon form other bonds that led to that momentous partnership. William Cullen Bryant had already begun the work that Olmsted and Vaux would eventually complete.[1] Bryant was not only one of America's

Above: Kindred Spirits *(1849), by Asher B. Durand, depicts two important figures, painter Thomas Cole and his friend the poet and journalist William Cullen Bryant, whose work contributed to the eventual creation of Central Park.*

Right: The Loch in the Ravine is a scene in Central Park created to resemble the natural landscape of the Catskills, depicted in paintings such as Kindred Spirits.

Frederick Law Olmsted (left) and Calvert Vaux (right), the codesigners of Central Park.

most famous Romantic poets but also the editor of the *New-York Evening Post*. He had proposed a park in an editorial on the eve of July 4, 1844. Complaining that New Yorkers had no open space in which to celebrate the national holiday, he urged civic leaders to take the land for a public park before commercial interests possessed every last inch of Manhattan Island.[2] For four more years, Bryant's call went unheeded. Due to the social unrest caused by the arrival in the city of the first Irish and German immigrants, New Yorkers were not ready for a public park.

The celebrated Hudson River estate designer and taste-maker Andrew Jackson Downing succeeded Bryant as the new voice for a park. In October 1848, he published his first article urging New Yorkers to develop spacious parks like those in Europe.[3] It is most likely that, given his prominence and connections, Downing and his young English-born protégé, architect Calvert Vaux, would have designed New York's future park. Downing was already engaged by President Millard Fillmore to design a large public park connecting the Capitol and the White House in Washington,

D.C., when, tragically, he became the victim of a fatal accident. He was on his way to New York when the engine of his steamboat exploded in a drag race with another vessel. The thirty-six-year-old designer drowned in the Hudson River trying to save the lives of other passengers. It fell to Vaux, his devoted protégé, to identify Downing's body.

Continuing Downing's architectural business in upstate Newburgh, Vaux became part of a circle of artists whose paintings of the picturesque landscape of the Hudson River Valley would make a lasting emotional impression on the future designer of Central Park. Downing's democratic values and social vision for public parks also influenced Vaux. The Englishman would later refer to Central Park as "the big art work of the Republic."[4]

In 1856, Vaux moved to New York City with his new bride, Mary McEntee, the sister of Hudson River painter Jervis McEntee. He established a successful architectural practice and began to make important personal and professional contacts. One of his first city commissions was for the home and bank of John A. C. Gray, one of the new state-appointed commissioners of Central Park. It was through Gray and another commissioner, Charles Wyllys Elliott, that Vaux learned about the plans for the new Central Park by Colonel Egbert Ludovicus Viele. Engineer-in-chief Viele was not only a West Point graduate and a specialist in mapping and sanitary drainage, he was also responsible for creating the design for the Park that had been adopted by the former Democrat-controlled and city-appointed commissioners, who had since been ousted by the new Republican-controlled and state-appointed ones.

Viele was quite knowledgeable about landscape design history and theory. Unfortunately, he was neither an artist nor a draftsman who could translate aesthetic and intellectual concepts into a convincing and well-designed plan. So when Calvert Vaux, a sensitive designer and talented architect, looked at the engineer's weakly realized plan for the future Park, he was justifiably horrified.

Vaux lost no time in convincing the new board of commissioners that Viele's plan was essentially no plan at all and that for such an important civic work—the cause for which Downing had fought so ardently—the commissioners

must hold a design competition. At that point, the well-positioned Vaux must have silently resolved to become Central Park's chosen designer. He had practiced architecture and landscape design with Downing and had a firm grasp of English landscape principles and theories. But he would need a plan. And he would need a partner.

When thirty-five-year-old Frederick Law Olmsted was appointed the superintendent of the new park on September 11, 1857, no one—himself included—could have imagined that day would launch the career of America's first, and to this day most renowned, landscape architect. Olmsted had been a restless spirit, jumping from one venture to another—his indulgent father, a successful dry-goods merchant in Hartford, Connecticut, kindly footing the bill.

Each of Olmsted's ventures reflected his love of the land. He had been a gentleman farmer, owning one farm in Connecticut and later another on Staten Island. He had published books on his travels in England and the plantations of the South, which discussed landscape directly and indirectly.[5] Having just failed in a publishing venture, Olmsted was quietly editing one of his books at an inn on the Connecticut shore when he ran into a friend, the newly appointed commissioner Charles Wyllys Elliott (coincidentally a friend to Downing and Vaux), who told him of the available position for superintendent of the new park. Olmsted was on the next boat to New York to pursue the job that would, in time, change both his life and the American landscape forever.

John Olmsted instilled a love and appreciation of landscape in his young son Frederick, creating the foundation for his future career as a landscape architect. While still very young, Frederick traveled with his father on horseback to admire picturesque scenery in the Connecticut countryside. Years later the famous designer acknowledged his father's devotion to scenery, saying that, "his sensitivity to the beauty of nature was indeed extraordinary . . . he gave more time and thought to the pursuit of this means of enjoyment than to all other luxuries."[6]

Olmsted's "loitering journeys" and "afternoon drives on the Connecticut meadows" were leisure-time pursuits popular with many well-to-do and middle-class people. Scenic tourism, or sightseeing, a form of travel that is still popular today, began in the eighteenth century with Europeans touring the countryside in pursuit of scenes like those that hung on the walls of their drawing rooms. Tourists often traveled with a Claude glass, a small pocket device whose convex glass reflected the chosen landscape onto a mirror. Today we capture such scenes with a camera. In the way that we invoke master photographer Ansel Adams when we are before a magnificent vista of Yosemite, the Americans of the 1850s would equate scenes of Kaaterskill Falls or Lake George with famous paintings by popular American artists.[7]

One hundred years before the paintings of the Hudson River School helped foster the creation of Central Park, European paintings by Frenchmen Claude Lorrain and Nicolas Poussin and the Italian Salvator Rosa influenced landscape designers who were creating similar compositions for the country estates of the English aristocracy. The writer and poet Alexander Pope expressed this kinship of the two arts succinctly: "All gardening is landscape painting. Just like a landscape hung-up." Two styles of naturalistic landscape design evolved—the pastoral and the picturesque—and both would come to characterize Central Park's landscapes.

The creation of pastoral landscapes developed in England in the eighteenth century with "landscape improvers" such as Lancelot "Capability" Brown. Geometric gardens that were planned by the obvious hand of man—Versailles being the most famous example—gradually gave way to landscapes that more closely evoked the hand of Mother Nature. The landscape at Blenheim, for example, once had straight walks and embroidered parterres, but under Brown's naturalistic redesign, the estate simulated the England of yore—broadly rolling hills, artfully placed clumps of trees, a gently sloping greensward, and sensuously contoured water bodies.[8]

The picturesque-landscape movement developed out of a reaction to the pastoral by late-eighteenth-century theorists such as William Gilpin in his tour books of Britain and Sir Uevedale Price in *Essays on the Picturesque*—two writers who greatly influenced Olmsted and Vaux. Gilpin and Price abhorred the quiet blandness of rolling green lawns.

Instead they advocated texture and drama in the landscape—the rough and rugged qualities of rock outcrops, gnarled trees, brooks and brushwood, rutted roads, and crumbling ruins that were best featured in the paintings of Salvator Rosa. Price promoted landscapes that would provoke a gamut of human emotions, associate the visitor with the Romantic history and literature of the past, and excite the viewer's curiosity in the intricacy and variety of nature. Picturesque scenery in landscape design is meant to stir a sense of mystery, intrigue, and delightful surprise as one moves through a series of artfully composed spaces. These were valuable lessons that Olmsted and Vaux would bring to the design of Central Park.

The topography of hills and valleys created by the outcrops of Manhattan schist on the pre-Park site lent itself to the picturesque style of landscape design developed in eighteenth-century England.

View from Summit Rock, [Central Park] looking West.
The Hudson River and Palisades.

Like most educated Americans, engineer Egbert Viele was no stranger to the ideas and traditions of European landscape design. In addition to his technical knowledge of topographic mapping and drainage, he had familiarized himself with popular English landscape gardening styles and theories. In his written description of "The Plan" in the *First Annual Report for the Improvement of the Central Park*, in January 1857, Viele explained the two design alternatives: the "ancient," which he described as "a desire to make nature assume a strictly artificial appearance, giving to every scene an air of formality and symmetry, a seeming attempt to apply the rules of architecture to landscape," and the "modern, based upon the maxim that 'the greatest art is to conceal art.'"[9] Viele, like all students of

In his plan for Central Park, Egbert Viele was influenced by the English designer Humphrey Repton, who emphasized the importance of elevated views. Viele's curvilinear drive, "The Circuit," meandered through the Park to connect such high points as Summit Rock at 83rd Street (above) and Vista Rock at 79th Street, both features named by the engineer. Rather than stressing views within the Park, Viele was more interested in views to landmarks outside the Park, such as the Hudson River, the Palisades, and Long Island Sound.

77

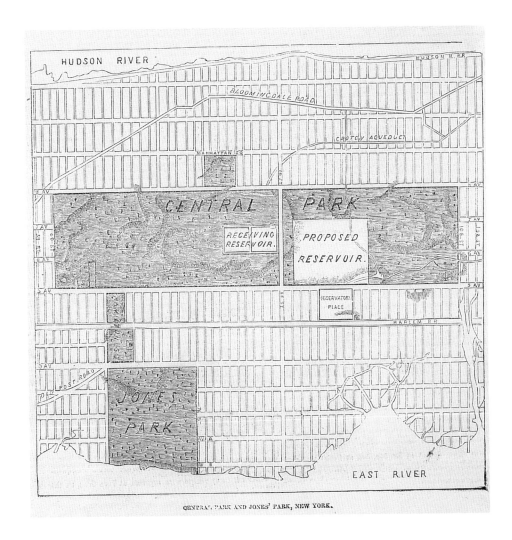

CENTRAL PARK AND JONES' PARK, NEW YORK.

the Romantic or "modern" school, rejected the T-square and looked to the "genius of the place" itself for cues to the future design:

> The hills, the valleys and the streams are nature's pencilings on the surface of the earth, rivaling, in their pictured grace, the most beautiful conceptions of the finite mind; to alter them, would be desecration; to erase them, folly! Upon a proper understanding of these features, and a proper appreciation of their beauty, depends the unity of the design.[10]

Viele contributed two very important features of the present Park. First, he decided to change the rectangular shape of the upper reservoir that was about to be constructed behind the existing, rectangular lower reservoir. Suggesting to name the new water body either Lake Manhatta or Croton Lake, Viele softened the edges, adding a more naturalistic outline to the billion-gallon receiving tank. Equally as important, Viele was also responsible for having created the concept of "certain transverse roads, at convenient distances, to allow of an easy transit across the

Park, for business and other purposes."[11] He placed the roads in their current locations, based on the natural configurations of the topography. When the commissioners sat down to establish the stipulation for the design competition, they put Viele's suggestion for the transverse roads second only to their conservative budget limitations.

Opposite: If it had not been for Viele's intercession, the upper reservoir would have been a design nightmare—a second rectangle within the rectangle of the Park itself.

Above: An aerial view of the billion-gallon, 106-acre Reservoir.

Latting's Observatory, across from the 1853 Crystal Palace Exhibition on 42nd Street, provided New Yorkers with their first "skyscraper" view of the city. The commissioners of Central Park required an exhibition hall and an observatory for all competition entries. Many entries to the design competition, including the plan by George Waring (page 85), suggested placing the Crystal Palace in the new Park. The Crystal Palace burned down in October, 1858. In the following year Latting offered his tower to the commissioners for Central Park, but his offer was rejected.

It is hard to please all of the people all of the time, but the commissioners were trying to do just that when in October 1857 they stipulated the requirements for the new park. Then, just as today, many New Yorkers wanted a park for sports and active recreation, particularly for cricket and the newly emerging game of "base-ball." Therefore, the commissioners requested that each plan have three playgrounds from three to ten acres.

For most New Yorkers, ice skating was also a desired activity. New York's rivers were too deep to freeze over and there was no large freshwater lake on which to skate during the winter months. Interestingly, the commissioners requested that an area "flowing with water to form a winter skating ground" be reserved, but they did not insist on the creation of a permanent lake. Perhaps they thought that constructing a man-made water body would have been too expensive; aesthetically, several commissioners considered the two vast reservoirs to be sufficient bodies of water for a park.

New York did not have an adequate parade ground for the state militia to drill and practice upon, and a park was seen by many as the opportunity to provide for that most important civic function. An important proposed feature of Central Park was to be "a parade ground of from twenty to forty acres" with "proper arrangements for the convenience for spectators."

In 1853, New York hosted the first American world's fair, the Crystal Palace Exhibition, fashioned after the success of the first modern global exposition in London held two years earlier. The display of international arts, crafts, and manufactured goods in a glass pavilion on the site of the future Bryant Park at Sixth Avenue and 42nd Street was so successful that it prompted the commissioners to require an exhibition and concert hall in the new park. The high point of the exhibition was Latting's Observatory, across the street from the exhibition hall, which gave New Yorkers their first "skyscraper" experience. The commissioners wanted to provide the public with thrilling views from a "prospect tower." Therefore, they mandated that each plan include an observatory.

A flower garden and a grand fountain, features found in most formal European parks, were to be included in each plan. Lastly, the financially conservative commissioners insisted that the construction of this grand and glorious park cost no more than $1.5 million. The commissioners offered $2,000 for the winning design, $1,000 for second place, $750 for third place, and $500 for fourth place.

THE COMPETITORS

For a true assessment of Olmsted and Vaux's winning entry, which they called the Greensward plan, it is important to understand its relationship to the other surviving submissions. The written descriptions accompanying the thirty-three plans indicate that almost all entries, like that of Egbert Viele, favored "modern" Romantic landscape design. They mention the broken, rocky, and swampy topography as best suited to the varied treatment of the picturesque aesthetic rather than either a pastoral or formal geometric design. Until recently, only three illustrative documents were known to exist: Viele's plan, which was first published in the 1857 *Annual Report;* future Park engineer George Waring's blueprint of his original plan, in the collection of the Frances Loeb Library, Graduate School of Design, Harvard University; and the nine-foot, ink-on-linen Greensward plan, which is on display in the conference room at the Arsenal, the headquarters of the New York City Department of Parks and Recreation, located in Central Park.[12]

Two more plans have come to light recently and are now available for study. Entry #30 by Samuel I. Gustin, whose proposal won second place in the competition, included a line drawing that was folded into his written description. Entry #4 by John J. Rink, an exquisitely preserved nine-foot watercolor, was recently discovered in an attic.

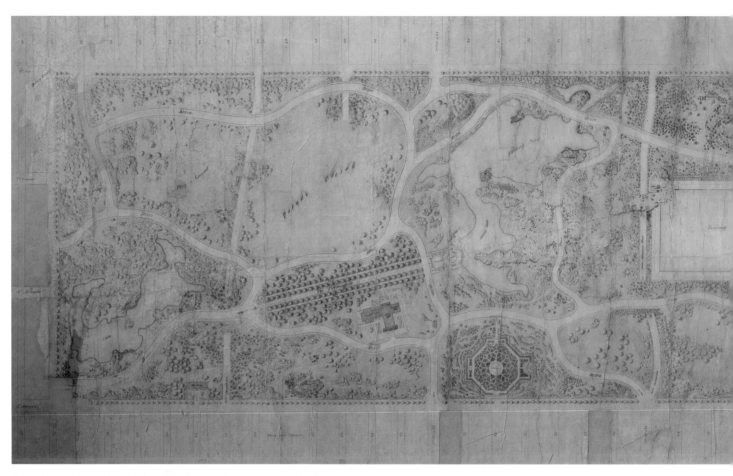

Frederick Law Olmsted and Calvert Vaux's prizewinning entry #33, the Greensward plan.

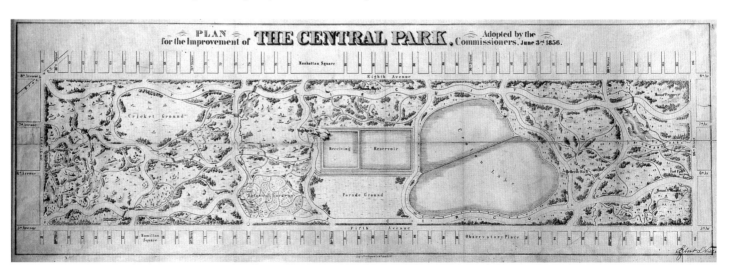

The first design for Central Park by engineer Egbert Viele was reentered as plan #28.

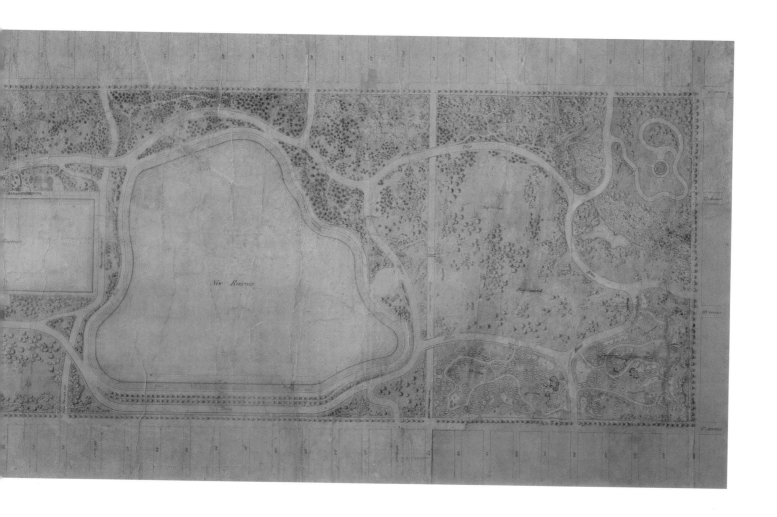

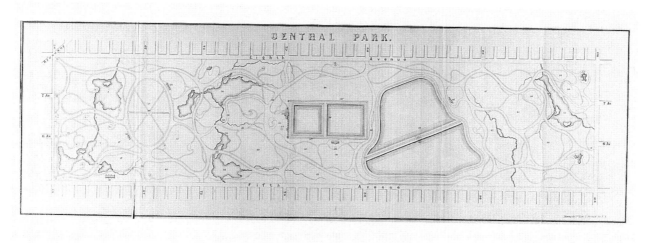

Second-place prize went to Samuel I. Gustin's plan, entry #30, published here for the first time.

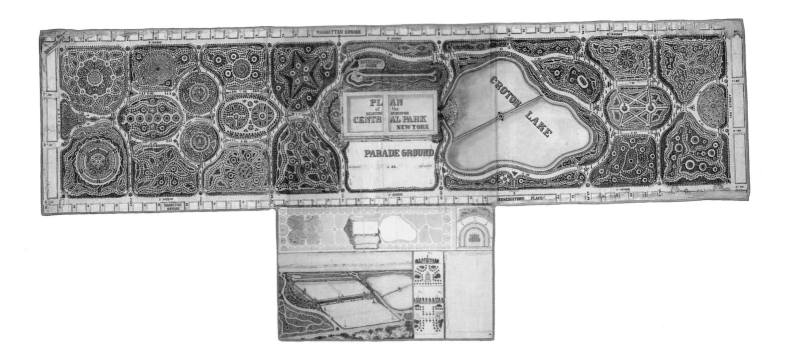

Entry #4 by John J. Rink, a graduate
of Cooper Union's engineering program, fantasized a landscape of
geometric gardens and topiary
plantings. Rink gave considerable
prominence to the military in his
competition entry. He placed the
required parade ground and a
museum on the site of the future
Metropolitan Museum of Art and
also included an artillery shooting
ground, which was not one of the
requirements. Rink also sunk a
small section of the required 86th
Street transverse road to pass
under his conception for a reservoir
cascade—resembling to a small
degree the much more expansive
vision of Olmsted and Vaux.

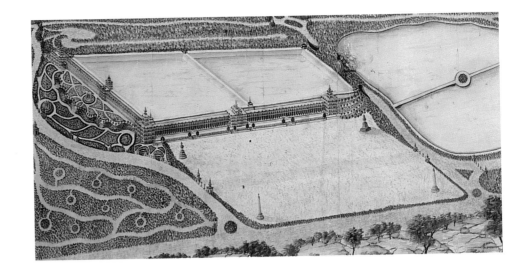

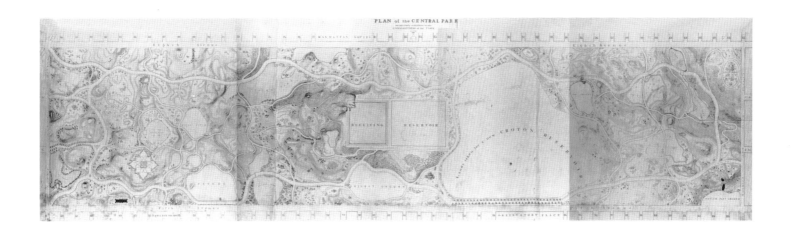

THE MISSING RINK

Lightly penciled on the reverse side of Rink's wildly fantastic nine-foot watercolor is the number four, verifying that it is indeed entry #4 to the Central Park competition. The plan is a detailed tapestry of curliqued stars, spirals, circles, and mazes, a series of small, unrelated topiary gardens that were common at the time.[13] Of real interest today is not so much Rink's design—although he did sink a small section of the 86th Street transverse road below grade as it passed under his proposed reservoir cascade—but rather his emphasis on the Park as a memorial to America's political and military history. A Cooper Union graduate in engineering who would later serve in the Army's engineering corps during the Civil War, Rink named his roads, drives, and gates after presidents, patriots, and signers of the Declaration of Independence: George Washington, John Adams, Thomas Jefferson, Alexander Hamilton, John Hancock, Benjamin Franklin, Robert Livingston, Thomas Mifflin, and Charles Pinckney; and Revolutionary War generals: Philip Schuyler, Anthony Wayne, Daniel Morgan, Israel Putnam, Nathanael Greene, and [Charles or Henry] Lee. Conceived as it was at a time of national crisis, Rink's submission, though unrealistic, seriously underscored the importance of and preoccupation with the principles of the nation, symbolized by its founders and its heroes.

Above: Park engineer George Waring's plan, entry #29, "Art, the Handmaiden of Nature." Waring became the Park's superintendent of draining.

Below: A few competition renderings by Roswell Graves, entry #25, have survived. In his plan for the main entrance at 59th Street, the Park engineer proposed an unimaginative maze of paths and small planting beds—a design treatment similar to those of home gardens and small urban squares.

The more credible of the newly discovered plans is that of Samuel Gustin, the second-place winner, who had been an important player in the choice for the site of the future park. In 1852, two sites on Manhattan Island were selected: Jones Wood, a 150-acre wooded and mature landscape from 63rd Street to 73rd Street along the East River, and a centrally located, swampy and rocky tract of 750 acres between 59th Street and 106th Street. When a special committee was formed to investigate the pros and cons of both locations, they chose expert horticulturists to assess their suitability. Gustin, a nurseryman from Newark, New Jersey, testified in a letter, reprinted in the 1852 majority report, that planting young trees in the somewhat barren central site was preferable to thinning the already mature stand of trees in Jones Wood.[14]

Once "the Central Park" site was chosen and under construction in 1857, Gustin was awarded the position of superintendent of planting, working under Viele. In the design competition held six months later, three of the four Democratic commissioners voted for Gustin's plan for first prize.

Though his plan did not propose the sunken transverse roads, Gustin did include a feature that many have considered the brainchild of Olmsted and Vaux: the three separate modes of circulation—carriage drive, bridle trail, and pedestrian path—an element used on the Avenue de l'Impératrice at the entryway to the Bois de Boulogne in Paris. Gustin included this important safety measure in his plan as well as a written description of the Bois de Boulogne authored by J[ean-Pierre] Barillet, Chief Architect of the Bois de Boulogne and Gardener for the Squares and Gardens for the City of Paris.[15]

Gustin's plan also included many features or suggestions that were either similar to those proposed in the Greensward plan or adopted at a later time: curvilinear drives, picturesque scenery, rustic benches and cascades, an Italian terrace, a lake at 59th Street, a large naturalistic lake crossing west to east near 72nd Street, the masking out of the reservoir walls with vegetation, the placement of the parade ground on the west side, the planting out of the perimeter, the damming up of McGowan's stream for "a Pool" in the north end, an arboretum, a pinetum, an observatory on the site of the Great Hill, a sequence of meadows on the site of the North Meadow, and a bridle trail that circled the future reservoir.

Though much more sophisticated than Viele's layout, Gustin's plan is, nonetheless, an inferior design to that of the first-place Greensward plan. It does not commit to the vast reorganization of land forms necessary to create the balance between the open meadows and water bodies and the intricate woodlands. Gustin's design, like Waring's, is chopped up into small sections of equal size, forming a patchwork of small streams, ponds, and glades arranged between the rock outcrops, as opposed to the dramatic juxtaposition of the infinite and the intimate that defines Olmsted and Vaux's grand symphonic vision.

OLMSTED AND VAUX, VAUX AND OLMSTED

Much to Olmsted's surprise, Calvert Vaux, whom he barely knew, suggested that they enter the design competition together.[16] The two men had met only once at Downing's home many years before, though they traveled in similar New York circles. Although Olmsted had spent his life admiring European parks, he never would have entered the competition on his own. As both a gentleman and Viele's faithful employee, he would have considered his boss's preferential standing. Olmsted—probably after much behind-the-scenes prodding from Vaux—respectfully asked Viele if he had any objections to his submitting a design. True to his contemptuous and difficult personality, the engineer-in-chief expressed complete indifference to his subordinate's polite consideration. With Viele's feelings out of the picture, Vaux was free to make his dream a reality, and the famous Olmsted and Vaux partnership began.

The lifelong friendship and on-again-off-again professional relationship between Olmsted and Vaux took root between October, 1857 and April 1, 1858, when the partners submitted the last—and late—entry #33 to the board of commissioners. Throughout those six months, they spent many moonlit nights walking the blank canvas of their future picture—a picture that was born out of their mutual attachment to the landscapes of their respective homelands.

The two men were indeed kindred spirits when it came to their appreciation of both the English and the American countrysides. Vaux's native homeland instilled in him the

Olmsted and Vaux named their plan "Greensward" from the English word for "unbroken stretches of turf or lawn." Nothing appears to be more natural than the rolling countryside of Cedar Hill. The landscape was fashioned, however, by covering a steep, rock slope with a cover of green lawn and blasting rock from the area below to imitate a natural meadow.

love of the pastoral—the green, rolling hills and broad, placid lakes—while his first home in his newly adopted country was the wildly picturesque landscape of Cole's Catskills and Church's Hudson River Valley. Olmsted, on the other hand, was raised to appreciate the rugged American landscape, though emotionally and temperamentally he seems to have preferred, above all else, the green pastures of Vaux's England. They named their plan "Greensward"—an English term that means "unbroken stretches of turf or lawn"—after their most desired type of landscape for New York's park.

THE GREENSWARD VISION

The narrow, rocky, and uneven topography of the rectangular site was better suited to the maze of small, pocket-size, picturesque landscapes and gardens that characterized the plans of Waring, Viele, and Gustin—and even to Rink's series of small topiary fantasies—than to the Greensward plan. Olmsted and Vaux also recognized the limitations of the ground, explaining that their "primary object in the design [was] to get the better of this most conspicuous defect of the site, and to take the utmost advantage of such opportunities . . . to make the visitor feel as if a considerable extent of country were open before him."[17]

The majority of submissions, including the Greensward plan, proposed enlarging the natural creek that ran west to east from 77th to 72nd Streets. Olmsted and Vaux believed that "[n]ext to groves and greensward, a sheet of water is the most important element in the character of the scenery."[18] They understood the impact of viewing a water body of indeterminate size, as Vaux explained, "50 feet of water will give an idea of distance and of difficulty in passing it greater than 500 feet of ground will."[19] Only the Greensward plan attempted this ambitious vision, which emphasized the psychological benefits of expansive vistas and created the illusion of even greater space. That vision required the daring and foresight to rearrange the land on a scale that had not been equaled in an American landscape before Central Park.

THE NEW PSYCHOLOGICAL LANDSCAPE

Olmsted's personal preference for peaceful meadows and placid lakes may have come from the deepest needs of his troubled spirit. Throughout his long life, Olmsted endured bouts of severe depression. He experienced two nervous breakdowns during his work on Central Park. His fights with Controller Andrew Haswell Green for control of the Park were so emotionally debilitating that he was forced to take a rest cure from his work on the Park in the fall of 1859.

From his earliest years with his father, Olmsted looked to nature to soothe his soul. His biographer, Charles Beveridge, has noted the central importance he placed on healing: "Not aesthetic theory but the very health of the human organism became the touchstone of his art."[20] Olmsted strongly believed in the healing powers of nature, a philosophy that hearkens back to Ralph Waldo Emerson's statement that "[t]he land is the appointed remedy for whatever is false and fantastic in our culture."[21] For Olmsted, the most fundamental goal of the Greensward plan was to provide for visitors a psychological response evoked most often by viewing natural scenery.

Opposite top: Olmsted and Vaux intended the vast, open stretches of green lawn, such as Sheep Meadow, to provide visual and psychological relief to residents of the cramped and crowded city.

Opposite bottom: Central Park's soothing landscapes also offered a calm in the storm during the years of the Civil War. When E. & H. T. Anthony published a series of Central Park stereo cards in 1863, the conflict was at its peak. Wishing to give their troubled president a respite from death and destruction, the publishers mailed Lincoln a package of their Central Park scenes in hopes that the views of "these quiet visitors may sometimes afford you a relaxation from the turmoil and cares of office." This scene is of Cabinet Bridge—later known as Oak Bridge—in the Ramble. When seen with a hand-held viewer, the cards provide a three-dimensional image.

Upper left: An 1857 photograph from the Greensward presentation of pre-Park land that would become the Lake and the Ramble beyond.

Upper right: The proposed painted view of the Lake and the Ramble presented in the Greensward plan.

Lower left: A photograph of the Lake and the Ramble in the new Park.

Lower right: The Hernshead promontory, the Lake, and the Ramble today.

Above: View from the Terrace Site *(1858), painted by Calvert Vaux's brother-in-law, the Hudson River painter Jervis McEntee, depicts the pre-Park site of the future Lake and Ramble.*

Right: The same view, showing the Lake and the Ramble today.

Natural elements found in the
northern end of Central Park
included large rock outcrops,
native vegetation, and abundant
natural springs. Olmsted and
Vaux sought to maximize these
picturesque features in the Park's
woodlands, here showing the
existing conditions on what
became the Great Hill.

Taking their cues from the natural
features, Olmsted and Vaux created
this naturalistic grotto to hide the
water pipe that is, in actuality, the
source of the Gill stream in the
Ramble. The density and variety of
plantings that Olmsted created in
the woodlands evoked the appearance of untamed nature.

"The soft, smooth, tranquil surface of turf," which provided a sense of infinite space, was Olmsted's "antidote" to the confinement of the city. While others would appreciate the sublime in landscapes that produced awe, and even a sense of physical fright, by the majesty of natural elements—Niagara Falls and the Rocky Mountains, to name but two—Olmsted craved the soothing pastoral landscape of the 23rd Psalm: "He maketh me to lie down in green pastures and leadeth me beside the still waters, he restoreth my soul."[22]

Olmsted felt that landscapes appealed to either our childlike or our mature emotions. While for him the pastoral lakes and meadows were designed to evoke feelings of "rest, tranquility, deliberation and maturity," the picturesque woodlands—the play of lights and darks in indeterminate spaces, the lushness of subtropical vegetation, and the variegated textures of wood, water, and rock—were meant to excite "the childish playfulness and profuse careless utterance of Nature" and provide mystery, intrigue, and rapture in the visitor's mind.[23]

THE PEOPLE'S PARK

For both designers, different styles of landscape appealed to the psychological needs of the individual. Whereas a visitor could find peace and solitude in the private spaces of woodland shelters, small glades, and quiet coves, that same individual could also choose to fulfill social and gregarious pleasures on the Mall, the Terrace, and the paths closest to the carriage drives. Vaux, in particular, enjoyed the extroverted, gregarious aspects of a public park and its democratizing role as "the great art work of the republic." As a transplanted Englishman, Vaux embraced the American dream of a classless society, so much more possible in his adopted country than in the rigid class system of his native land.

As an architect, Vaux focused on people's social needs and their enjoyment of spectacle. Before starting to work on the design for Central Park, Vaux had already been promoting to other New York architects the then radical concept of the apartment building.[24] He saw the potential for multiple-unit dwellings as fulfilling the human need for socialization while also solving the problems of limited space in cities. Nonetheless, that notion would not be realized until Richard Morris Hunt's Stuyvesant Building was erected in 1869, as well-to-do and middle-class Americans insisted on living in private homes.[25] The shared spaces of Central Park were precursors of the future lifestyle of urban Americans.

Both Olmsted and Vaux jointly credited the partnership with their most innovative concept—the sunken transverse roads. However, at least one source—a biographical manuscript, authorized by Andrew Haswell Green—acknowledged Calvert Vaux as "especially" having the "idea and concept" for the innovation.[26] Nonetheless, despite the many disputes about their ideas for the Greensward plan, the two men remained steadfast to their joint contribution until the end of their lives.

The presentation pencil sketches and watercolor drawings of the Greensward plan—many of them signed by Vaux's eventual assistant, architect Jacob Wrey Mould—show a profusion of structures in a number of styles that Vaux and Mould adopted from contemporary architecture. The presentation drawings include a Venetian gondola beside a Turkish style kiosk on what is now Hernshead (see page 91), a Ruskinian Gothic red-and-white-striped brick observatory for the upper Park, an elaborate Moorish or Venetian Gothic shelter designed for baseball spectators on the lower playground, and an Italianate villa, designed for the required exhibition hall positioned above the "Italian terrace." A rounded classical temple—a structure found in Romantic English gardens—was envisioned for the top of Cherry Hill.

The ornamental bridges, perhaps the most defining architectural trait of Central Park, are absent in the Greensward plan, which featured only one rustic bridge in the north end of the Park. It would take muscle in both the field and the boardroom to turn Olmsted and Vaux's entry into the Central Park that we have come to know today.

Above: The Ruskinian Gothic observatory and pastoral landscape proposed for the Great Hill, with the Ravine below it. Though never built, it bears a resemblance to both the future tower on the Jefferson Market Courthouse, designed by Vaux and his partner Frederick Clarke Withers, and Mould's All Souls Unitarian Church that stood on Fourth Avenue and 20th Street.

Right: Vaux designed an ornate Venetian Gothic shelter on the top of the outcrop that overlooks the ball fields of the lower playground. Meant for the comfort of those watching the new game of "base-ball," the outcrop subsequently became known as Umpire Rock for the traditional role of the spectators. Mould depicted both the shelter and a ball game in progress in one of the charming presentation drawings.

*Above: Vaux and Mould designed
an elaborate bi-level Garden Arcade
for the proposed conservatory on
Fifth Avenue. The Romanesque
arches and sculpted figures were
eventually incorporated into Vaux's
plan for Bethesda Terrace by 1862.*

*Left: Vaux's original concept for
the "Italian terrace" only featured
one grand staircase, entered from
the drive. The connecting staircase from the Mall and the underground arcade were created only
when the bridges and arches were
later added to the design. Vaux
also envisioned an Italianate exhibition hall and a round, classical
temple for Cherry Hill—structures
that were never built.*

Winning first prize was just the beginning.

Olmsted and Vaux expected the details of

the design to evolve through collaboration

and compromise, taking into account the

topography of the land and the demands of

the commissioners, who represented the

public and controlled the purse strings.[1]

What they did not foresee, however, was a

forceful campaign in both the boardroom

and the press to modify the Greensward

plan almost to the point of its annihilation.

Brilliantly, the designers were able to pre-

serve the essence of their design while

devising inventive solutions to some of

the commissioners' more difficult demands. And in the end, the completed park became a more innovative and exciting creation than was proposed in the prize-winning plan. The constructed park was not the autocratic vision of a single artist and patron—such as Michelangelo and Pope Julius II for the Sistine Chapel, or Le Nôtre and Louis XIV at Versailles—but rather a synthesis of diverse opinions on appropriate park use, cultural expectations, and landscape styles that establishes Central Park as an American innovation, born out of a democratic process.

Dillon and Belmont

Two weeks after the announcement of the winners, Commissioner Robert J. Dillon—who, as corporation counsel to the City to New York, had been a forceful advocate for the adoption of the Park bill in 1853—proposed seventeen amendments to the Greensward plan, with many of his recommendations coming from other competition entries. In subsequent board meetings, Dillon's plan was backed by a fellow Democrat, August Belmont. Opposed to the naturalistic landscape aesthetic, the two men favored a more formal and geometric plan. Dillon had originally suggested that that the commissioners invite the designers of the Bois de Boulogne to consult on a plan for the Park even before the competition was announced, preferring the older European style of landscape design that focused on one grand, commanding feature. To Dillon and Belmont, this feature was one long and straight line. Beginning in the middle of 59th Street, their grand "Cathedral avenue," a straight mile-long boulevard, resembled fourth-place winner Howard Daniels's proposal for a similar "Central Avenue."[2] Continuing the straight line over the Lake and Ramble, the avenue would then connect the two reservoirs via a suspension bridge—a feature proposed in a submission by Park surveyors Charles Graham and John Bagley. After a promenade around the two reservoirs, a second suspension bridge would carry the visitor north over the Ravine to the top of the Great Hill, returning south via the same route.

Above: The curvilinear drives were designed by Olmsted and Vaux to prevent horseback and carriage racing. Park rules set the speed limit to seven miles per hour.

Opposite: The meandering five-and-a-half-mile bridle trail resembles a secluded country lane.

Dillon and Belmont were emotionally and financially invested in New York City as the leader of a new technological age, and they promoted the Park as a showcase for feats of engineering such as the suspension bridge.[3] They rejoiced in New York's state-of-the-art Croton water system and considered the reservoirs "the jewels of the Park," symbolizing "the wealth, the enterprise, the science and the sagacity of the people of New York."[4] The Romantic plan of Olmsted and Vaux also relied on advanced technology for its success, but whereas their concept purposely chose to blur the fine line between natural and naturalistic, the overtly formal plan of Dillon and Belmont preferred to impose that fine line straight up the middle of the Park.

In their penchant for technological advancement, however, it is ironic that these two commissioners wanted to eradicate the sunken transverse roads, which are the prototype for our modern highway system. For all their business acumen, Dillon and Belmont had a limited vision of the city's future, falsely predicting there would be "little or no such business relations of one side [of the city] with the other" to require roads through the Park.

August Belmont's passion for horseback and carriage riding influenced the ultimate design of the Park. As the owner of the finest stable of thoroughbred horses in the country, he was the future founder of both the Jockey Club and the Belmont Stakes—still one of the world's great races. It is no surprise, therefore, that Belmont wanted a bridle trail that looped around the entire Park. For this reason he preferred Samuel Gustin's second-place plan, which

incorporated both a separate park-wide bridle trail *and* a race track. Gustin envisioned a road surrounding a thirty-five-acre parade ground, "prepared especially with reference for equestrianism, particularly advantageous for trials of speed, displays of horsemanship, and the like."[5]

Olmsted and Vaux restricted their "Ride" or bridle trail to a mere mile-and-a-half circuit around the new reservoir, inadequate for horseback riders wishing to ride through the entire Park. The limitless meadows and abundant woodlands that defined the Greensward plan afforded no room for a lengthy bridle trail within the narrow confines of the half-mile-wide site. Olmsted and Vaux purposely designed their curvilinear drives to be shared by both horseback riders and carriages in order to prevent the possibility of "trotting matches."[6] Dillon and Belmont, who wanted both safety for all Park users and an extensive bridle trail, fought for the most important feature of Gustin's plan—the complete separation of the bridle trail from pedestrian paths and carriage drives—a scheme mistakenly attributed to the original Greensward plan.

Determined to get their way, Dillon and Belmont took their cause to the people, placing their seventeen amendments in the major metropolitan newspapers. The well-connected Olmsted fought back by taking New York's most powerful newspapermen to the undeveloped site to view the damage that Dillon and Belmont's proposed changes would do to the letter and spirit of the Greensward plan. The debate was followed closely by the public, who had the opportunity to view all thirty-three plans in an open exhibition—a suggestion of the public-minded commissioner Andrew Haswell Green.

In the end, it was the support from a coalition of the remaining commissioners and Olmsted's powerful press connections that saved the essence of the Greensward plan. Nonetheless, the board granted Belmont and Dillon's wish for both the extended bridle trail and the complete separation of ways that was so necessary for an anxiety-free park experience. In the years to come, the innovative solution they devised for the separation of ways would become a hallmark of all Olmsted and Vaux parks.

The Bridges

Dillon's demands sent Olmsted and Vaux back to their drawing boards. By September 1858, the designers accommodated the longer bridle trail and separate systems of traffic by introducing into the plan ornamental bridges and arches that allowed for the additional roadways. They became signature features of Central Park.

The material and design of each bridge were intended to harmonize with its respective landscape: the expensive Marble Arch for the subterranean entranceway to the formal Mall (see page 24); decorative brick, limestone, or brownstone within the pastoral areas; filigree cast-iron ornamentation for the bridle trail; and unmilled locust or cedar timber and rough-hewn stone, blasted from the rock outcrops, in the woodlands.

Our appreciation for the beauty and craft of the Park's bridges and arches is a modern sensibility. Surprisingly, the designers intended them to disappear under a thick cover of vines so they would fuse with the naturalistic landscape. Yet today we delight in these structures, such as this stone arch in the Ramble, as first-rate examples of Vaux and Mould's creativity.

Woven throughout the Park, Vaux's thirty-nine arches and bridges—no two alike—added elegance and texture to the rural landscape.

Attributed to Jacob Wrey Mould, the original design for Gapstow Bridge over the Pond at 59th Street resembled contemporary railway bridges.

103

Left: Bridge no. 28, sometimes called "Gothic Bridge," is one of the three cast-iron bridges over the Reservoir bridle trail.

Top: Trefoil Arch at Conservatory Water is made of brownstone.

Above: Inscope Arch at the Pond is made of pink granite.

Above: Pinebank Arch at the southernmost end of the bridle trail.

Right: Bow Bridge, the most famous span in the Park, owes its existence to Commissioner Dillon's desire for a suspension bridge. Olmsted and Vaux intended the Ramble to feel physically and psychologically remote from the Terrace, though in actuality the distance between them was less than the length of an average city block. They wanted visitors to amble slowly around the east or west paths of the Lake to reach the Ramble, rather than cross a bridge between the two landscapes. As a compromise to Dillon, the designers constructed the low-lying bridge. Named for its resemblance to an archer's bow, it immediately became one of Central Park's most cherished icons.

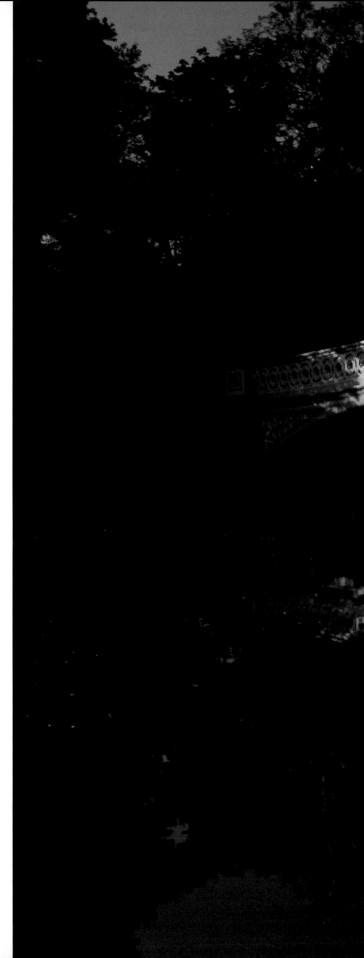

Right: Rustic bridges of unmilled timber are used in the woodlands, such as this example over the Loch in the Ravine.

Opposite: Glen Span Arch is typical of the rustic stonework created for the woodlands. The boulders were made from blasting the outcrops during construction of the Park.

The Pastoral Park: Meadows

The Park was meant, literally and figuratively, to be a moving experience. Indeed, no single photograph can capture completely the designers' intentions. Visitors were meant to pass through it, unable to take it all in at a single glance. The notion of "passages of scenery," as Olmsted called the experience of passing through the various "pictures," is as evident in each individual landscape as it is throughout the Park.

THE NORTH MEADOW

The designers' intention for a limitless greensward, combined with the experience of moving through space, is best experienced today in the butterfly-shape North Meadow. Walking across the east or west drive, we are drawn toward the hint of a distant meadow through a screen of trees. Once we cross the border, a broad, undulating expanse of turf unfolds before us. Stretching from 97th Street to 102nd Street, the meadow feels much longer than its five city blocks. As we walk either east or west, the meadow narrows, and a small tree-capped hillock juts into the middle of the scene; a hazy line of treetops is visible in the distance. Beyond this promontory, the meadow springs open once again to reveal another great expanse of lawn, edged by rock outcrops and groves of magnificent trees. On a sunny, day-long visit, the play of light and shadow slowly shifts the composition, sharp and clear by day, hazy and indistinct against the setting sun.

The butterfly-shape North Meadow comes closest to the designers' intended experience of a limitless meadow. The rock outcrops that remained in the landscapes after blasting were left purposely to act as sculptural design elements, giving Central Park its distinct character.

THE SHEEP MEADOW

Today the tall and tight ring of trees that encircles the fifteen-acre meadow prevents visitors from appreciating the sense of limitless space so essential to Olmsted and Vaux's rural vision. The composition of the original meadow and its surrounding landscape provided the visitor with ample space between the artfully placed trees to glimpse northward to the western portion of the Lake and southward, across the invisible transverse road, to the connecting meadow—now Heckscher Ball Field and Playground.

The breadth of this quintessential pastoral sequence—the most expensive one in the Park to construct—provided the nineteenth-century visitor with a mile-long view from 62nd Street to 79th Street.

Walking barefoot on the luxurious green grass is one of the great delights of the Sheep Meadow today. This pleasure was inaccessible to nineteenth-century visitors, who would have considered it unthinkable to walk barefoot in public. Furthermore, visitors to the Park were instructed to receive their "mental refreshment" just by *looking* at the pastoral picture, not by stepping into it. "Keep Off the Grass" signs prevailed. Commissioner Andrew Green stated the board's philosophy in 1863, "The blades of grass that united, make up a lawn, can be enjoyed without pressing them underfoot."[7] Referred to as "the Commons" or "the Green," the Sheep Meadow was open to the public only when signs announcing the time and place were posted.

Asking how the Sheep Meadow got its name is a little like asking who is buried in Grant's Tomb, and yet many people are surprised to learn that a flock of pedigree Southdown (and later Dorset) sheep inhabited the meadow from 1864 until 1934. The purpose of the sheep was twofold: one aesthetic and one practical. To the designers, nothing was more representative of the pastoral aesthetic than a flock of grazing sheep on a meadow. On the practical side, the sheep were the most cost-effective way to mow and fertilize the lawn. The sheep also provided revenue for the

Opposite: The fifteen-acre Sheep Meadow is the largest green in the Park, unencumbered by baseball diamonds and backstops that tend to diminish the pastoral effects intended by the designers.

Below: Although we celebrate the buildings surrounding the Park, the best time to experience the Sheep Meadow as it was in the nineteenth century is on a misty day, when the low cloud cover erases the city from view. At that time, the landscape draws you in, and a sense of breadth and depth replaces the boundary of the buildings on the perimeter.

From 1864 to 1934 a flock of
Southdown (later Dorset) sheep
pastured on "the Green" or "the
Commons." By the turn of the cen-
tury the landscape became known
as the Sheep Meadow.

Park in the way of lambs, breeders, and wool. The commissioners noted with great satisfaction, "the products of the sheep, which are so attractive as they graze upon the lawns, nearly pays the expense of their care and feeding."[8] There has been at least one account of a well-known, turn-of-the-century restaurant serving "selle d'agneau [saddle of lamb] de Central Park" on its bill of fare.

By the last decade of the nineteenth century, relaxation of the strict rules governing the accessibility of the Park's lawns slowly changed the Sheep Meadow from a picture-perfect pastoral landscape into a stage for the increasingly popular mass events that have made Central Park world-famous.

The Progressive movement of the early years of the twentieth century redefined the Park from a pastoral vision to a recreation space in order to assimilate the rising tide of immigrants and working-class people into American culture. Mere exposure to a beautifully kept lawn was still considered effective for soothing one's nerves, but woefully inadequate by itself for the inculcation of American values. Park managers now felt that human intervention in the guise of sports, political and cultural events, and organized extravaganzas—the larger the better—would be more effective.[9]

Above: Sheep were not the only animals caring for the meadow; camels from the zoo were hitched to mowing machines. We can attribute this concept to showman and entrepreneur P. T. Barnum, who not only loaned many of his exotic animals to the Central Park Menagerie but also had elephants mowing the lawn on his private Connecticut estate.

Left: From the 1930s to the 1960s the Sheep Meadow became the open-air stage for mass productions by New York City school students. In the 1960s it became the site of mass demonstrations against the Vietnam War, love-ins, be-ins, and famous concerts by Barbra Streisand and James Taylor.

Everyone remembers the famous concerts and events held on the Great Lawn, yet few know that this luxurious green oval at the geographical center of Central Park was also the center of tremendous conflict concerning the design and purpose of the Park itself.

The site of the present Great Lawn had been occupied by the old receiving reservoir since 1842. When the inevitable expansion of New York's water system was announced in the 1880s, it signaled the eventual destruction of the thirty-seven-acre facility and opened the way for the Park's second-biggest design war. By the 1910s New Yorkers already envisioned the "vacant" space as an opportunity for modernization. Airplane landing ports, radio towers, sports arenas, an opera house, underground parking garages, and even a mausoleum for the storage of motion pictures (proposed by William Fox, founder of Twentieth Century-Fox) were some of the suggestions for the precious site.

After the reservoir was drained in 1931 and rubble from the Rockefeller Center construction site began to fill the cavernous hole, arguments focused more on the use of the space. Social reformers wanted baseball fields and playgrounds while preservationists fought to preserve Olmsted and Vaux's rural retreat. A spokesperson in favor of recreational use attacked the Park as a precious work of art,

Mention Central Park to most people and they will invariably recall at least one famous performance or media event that happened on the Great Lawn. Popular music fans remember Diana Ross, Elton John, Simon and Garfunkel, or Paul Simon by himself. Classical music enthusiasts recall performances by the New York Philharmonic as well as Metropolitan Opera tenors Luciano Pavarotti, Placido Domingo, and José Carreras. Older New Yorkers might cite the pre-Delacorte Theatre days of free Shakespeare by Joseph Papp, while others will mention the appearances of Billy Graham and Pope John Paul II. In 1982 it was the site of an anti-nuclear rally, in 1988 a display of the AIDS quilt, and in 1995 the premiere of Disney's Pocahontas. The Great Lawn was restored in 1997.

exaggerating that the "issue was art on one side and boys and girls on the other."[10] In the end, those in favor of defending the greensward held the line, and a well-rounded compromise was formed with the construction of a green oval, the "Great Lawn for Play." It was proposed by the New York chapter of the American Society of Landscape Architects (ASLA), the professional organization whose founders in 1899 included the sons of Olmsted and Vaux.

Opened in 1937, a green lawn dominated the former reservoir space, while recreation areas were placed at the northern end. Baseball diamonds were introduced in the 1950s. Despite efforts by an ardent and passionate band of preservationists, recreation and sports were firmly entrenched in Central Park until the earth movement in the late 1970s influenced a shift in values, and the original vision of Central Park as a green oasis was favored. Today we once again appreciate the area's democratic spirit in embracing both active and quiet use.

Top: When the water system that fed the lower reservoir became obsolete, the landscape became the site of many proposed projects. One of them, a 1923 plan by Thomas Hastings (architect of the New York Public Library) for a memorial to the soldiers of World War I, would have retained the rectilinear walls of the lower reservoir as a reflecting pool surrounded by allées of geometrically shaped trees. For years Henry Fairfield Osborn, director of the American Museum of Natural History, advocated a similar landscape, which also proposed an east/west pedestrian and automobile "driveway" and boulevard similar to the Champs-Élysées in Paris. It would have connected the natural history museum to the Metropolitan Museum of Art, presided over by his brother, William Church Osborn.

Bottom: The New York Philharmonic has performed in Central Park since 1965. Turtle Pond, pictured in the foreground, is the home of turtles, dragonflies, and aquatic birds.

The Pastoral Park: Water

THE LAKE

The farthest edge of Bethesda Terrace was the site of a boat-rental concession for the first fifteen years of the Park's existence. A row across the twenty-two-acre butterfly-shape Lake, the largest naturalistic water body in the Park, is quite similar to the experience of walking across the North Meadow. The trip originally began at the Terrace, directly across from the Point, which juts out from the receding shore of the Ramble. To the west of the Point, the shore of the Ramble gently sweeps into an S-curve until, surprisingly, the graceful and elegant Bow Bridge comes into full view. This narrow passage of the Lake plays the same role as the knoll in the North Meadow, first condensing the space so that the next view springs open to a broad expanse—in this case, of placid water.

The single most important view in the Park was intended to be the one from Bethesda Terrace, where the pastoral Lake mediated between the formal architecture of the Terrace and the wildness of the woodland Ramble.

Above and right: The undulating shoreline of the Lake with its rock promontory of Hernshead.

Features at the water's edge teased the nineteenth-century visitor with the promise of adventures. Just to the west of the bridge, an island planted with vegetation that gave subtropical effects added to the experience of nature's bounty and the appreciation of global biodiversity. Along the eastern shore of this lobe of the Lake, rustic boat landings enticed visitors to alight and explore the secrets of the Ramble.

In the early years of the Park's existence, more than one hundred thousand people in a day and five hundred thousand in a week reportedly went to the Park for ice skating. At night calcium lamps would light up the ice around Bethesda Terrace, and the Park would be transformed into a magical wonderland. Prior to the 1860s, ice skates were expensive and owned only by the wealthy. Once the water bodies in the Park were opened for skating, however, skates could be purchased in city stores for twenty-five cents or rented in the Park. Poor children would earn money helping to fasten the skates on women, who had difficulty bending down in their voluminous dresses.

Opposite: The view from the Ramble looks west to Bow Bridge, which crosses the Lake at its narrowest point.

Above left: Hidden inlets and rustic boat landings, such as Wagner Cove at the southern end of the Lake, enchant unsuspecting rowers. In the nineteenth century passenger boats circulated the Lake, stopping at the six landings to pick up and discharge visitors.

Above right: Rowboats have been a popular attraction on the Lake since the early years of the Park.

Opposite: From the 1930s to 1950, before a rink was constructed, the Parks Department created a temporary ice-hockey area on the Pond at 59th Street when weather permitted.

Left: Artist Winslow Homer captured a lone female skater on Ladies Pond, a portion of the Lake that was reserved for unaccompanied women who preferred to practice the new sport without male spectators.

For the first decade of its existence, more people visited Central Park in the winter, for the novelty of ice-skating, than in the warmer months.

Above: The lights of the city create a magical backdrop for the Wollman Skating Rink. Located on a former arm of the 59th Street Pond, the rink guarantees ice-skating from late fall to early spring.

125

THE HARLEM MEER

When its boundaries were first established in 1853, the Park ended at 106th Street because city planners could not envision transforming a high wall of rock outcrops and the large swamp beyond into a scenic landscape without prohibitive expenditures. Nonetheless, in 1863 the additional acreage was given over to the Park, as it would have taken much more money to develop the area for commercial or residential purposes.

The Harlem Meer, recalling the Dutch word for lake, is the best fishing spot in the Park, and very possibly among the first waters in America to be used for sport fishing. British soldiers brought recreational fishing to the colonies during the Revolutionary War. From 1776 to 1783, when British soldiers were stationed near the natural trout streams and swamps in what became the upper Park, it is very likely that they fished with rods and reels, which would have been new to Americans.

Above: The northern end of Central Park was once a part of the village of Harlem. The designers named the upper lake the Harlem Meer, recalling the Dutch word for lake.

Right: The Harlem Meer is stocked with many species of freshwater fish, and catch-and-release fishing is available at the Charles A. Dana Discovery Center.

Opposite: There are more than twenty-six thousand trees in Central Park.
This page: The dazzling spring-bulb display at the entrance to the Park at 59th Street.

The Picturesque Park: Woodlands

The Ramble and the Ravine, the two main woodlands in
the Park, have similar features: dense woodland plantings,
placid streams, rushing cascades, bridges made from the
blasted rock, rustic wooden furniture, and such fantasy
constructions as the Cave in the Ramble, the Grotto at the
Pool, and Huddlestone Arch in the Ravine. As sequential
experiences, however, the Ramble is a scrambled maze
while the Ravine is a fluid line.

*Above: Much of the mystery and
"childish playfulness," using
Olmsted's words, evoked in the
woodlands were realized through
plantings of dense vegetation.*

*Opposite: The most mysterious
and fantastic feature in the
Ramble was the Indian Cave. The
designers created it when they
uncovered massive perpendicular
rocks. Once the boulders were*

*secured, the Cave became a major
attraction. From an inlet at the
southwestern shore of the Lake,
boats could glide to its mouth.
Visitors had the choice to either
ascend the steep flight of stairs cut
into the Cave's facade or walk
directly into the dark and mysterious crypt that ran under the pathway, exiting near the Ramble's
rustic stone arch. The Cave was
closed off in the 1920s.*

130

THE RAMBLE

The Ramble was and is still the most complex landscape in Central Park. Densely planted woods, a web of paths, fanciful rustic structures, jagged outcrops, a cave, and roller-coaster topography of sharp turns and steep angles create dramatic picturesque effects. Indeed, Olmsted intended an "intricate disposition of lights and shadows [to] create a degree of obscurity not absolutely impenetrable, but sufficient to affect the imagination with a sense of mystery."[11]

Though Olmsted and his superintendent of planting, Ignaz Pilat, knew they could not use actual tropical plants in New York's temperate climate, they created lush subtropical effects through artful compositions that extensively used shrubs and ground cover for their forms, textures, and colors. Writing to his gardeners, Olmsted communicated his aesthetic vision in the same way that a painter would instruct his studio assistants,

Reached by the twisting and turning paths of the Ramble, Azalea Pond is a pleasant and peaceful surprise. A rustic bridge and benches evoke a scene in the Adirondacks—the intent of the designers.

In these [woodlands] the surface should be more or less rough and rude, the trees and shrubs should grow in them, some standing up and some struggling along the ground; instead of a smooth turf surface of clean short grass there should be varied sorts of herbage one crowding over another and all running together without any order, or there should be vines and creepers and mosses and ferns.[12]

The tupelo, one of the most
magnificent trees in Central
Park, is a commanding autumn
feature in the Ramble.

THE POOL, THE RAVINE, AND THE LOCH MEADOW

The combination of the Pool and the Ravine is acknowledged as a stunning example of Olmsted and Vaux's landscape sequences. Therefore, it is rather interesting to learn that, once again, such an "Olmstedian" feature owes much of its design to Commissioner Dillon. The natural topography featured an abundant stream, known as Montayne's Rivulet,[13] which ran east by northeast across the future park. In their original Greensward plan, the designers proposed widening the confluence of this stream with a smaller one to the south to create a small pool on the site of the present Springbanks Arch, since they felt that "mere rivulets are uninteresting, and we preferred to collect the ornamental water in large sheets."[14] In his famous list of seventeen amendments, however, Dillon specified a much larger lake, similar in scope and design to the one proposed by his favored entrant, Samuel Gustin.[15]

Above: The Pool is the most intimate water body in the Park, tucked below the steep embankment of Central Park West between 100th and 103rd Streets.

Opposite: Glen Span Arch looking toward the Pool and the first cascade. The Park's arches act as frames for the landscapes, similar to the frames of paintings.

Furthermore, Dillon suggested a cascade be formed from the water that would spill over the wall of the dam, which was constructed to create the Pool. There is no record of any protest about this particular amendment, so Olmsted and Vaux reconfigured the stream into as large a sheet of water as they could construct at the site. Unlike the larger water bodies—the Lake, the Pond, and the Meer—the Pool is small enough to be taken in at a single glance. The trees surrounding the Pool are particularly brilliant in autumn, but even the site has a quiet serenity that makes each visitor feel as though it is his or her own secluded resting place.

At the eastern end of the Pool visitors are lured into a steep and narrow space by the sound of rushing water—the twenty-foot cascade. Below the cascade is the first glimpse of the Loch, the brook that threads itself through the eye of Glen Span Arch. Beyond the sunlit and open Pool, a stairway of boulders descends alongside the rushing waterfall.

Left: Through the grottolike Glen Span Arch is a hushed woodland crossed by a placid stream known as the Loch. The woodland waterways attract aquatic birds such as the snowy egret.

Above: Central Park is one of the richest and most popular birding spots in North America due to New York's location on the Atlantic Flyway migratory route. In 1989, the late Roger Tory Peterson (center), author and illustrator of the world's most authoritative birding guidebooks, came back to Central Park, one of his favorite boyhood birding sites, for a bird-watching tour.

Opposite: Behind this rustic bridge, a dam creates a secret cascade with the most graceful spillway in the Park.

Above: Dropping at least fifteen feet, the Huddlestone Cascade is the most spectacular waterfall in Central Park. It is constructed so naturally that one can hardly believe it is entirely man-made.

Top: Vaux's Huddlestone Arch, created from massive boulders that were blasted during the Park's construction, can be seen either as a bridge about to crumble or, conversely, a rock outcrop put back together again Humpty Dumpty style. The arch is a true testament to the laws of gravity, as no mortar was used in its construction; only the weight of the stones "huddling" against one another keeps the arch standing.

Above and right: Carpeted by tall grasses and wildflowers, the naturalistic meadow adjacent to the Loch is maintained as the only woodland meadow in the Park.

SHAKESPEARE GARDEN

Though not an original feature of the Greensward plan, the Shakespeare Garden is Central Park's equivalent of a charming cottage garden. It is adjacent to the Swedish Cottage, once Sweden's entry to the 1876 Centennial Exhibition in Philadelphia and now a marionette theater. In 1915 Park Commissioner Charles Stover dedicated the garden to Shakespeare in honor of his recently departed friend Mayor Gaynor, a passionate devotee of the Bard.

In 1880, before the site became the Shakespeare Garden, a black mulberry from Stratford-on-Avon was planted. It can still be seen arching over the western entrance to the garden. In 1917 an oak tree from Stratford-on-Avon was planted along with other seeds and cuttings, and in 1932 a rose bush from Stratford was added.

Above: A visitor to Central Park, this richly colored pheasant blends in with the spring flowers at the Shakespeare Garden. In the early 1860s pheasant, as well as many other exotic birds, were placed in the Park. Private citizens released sparrows, a practice continued by Park administrators. In 1890 and 1891 New York businessman Eugene Schieffelin released starlings into the Park, the beginning of his plan to introduce into America all the birds mentioned in the works of Shakespeare.

Opposite: Bronze plaques bearing Shakespearean quotes about plants are placed near the appropriate flowerbeds. At one time a bust of the Bard was featured in the garden.

The rustic benches, wood and wattle fencing, and vine-woven flower guards in the Shakespeare Garden evoke Elizabethan gardens.

145

The Formal Park: Gardens

CONSERVATORY WATER

Olmsted and Vaux considered the sequence of the Mall and Bethesda Terrace the only important formal landscape in their design, though the competition insisted on the inclusion of a formal flower garden. The designers chose the present Conservatory Water site, along Fifth Avenue, for their garden. However, several other design entries—Gustin's and Waring's included—suggested a small pond at this site, where several small streams collected. This plan was also preferred by Commissioner Dillon. In another compromise, Olmsted and Vaux created a formal, hard-edged pool instead of a naturalistic water body, still intending to build a conservatory at the site.[16] The pool became known unofficially as the Model Boat Pond, where dedicated hobbyists still launch and race miniature yachts and sailboats today.

Commissioner Robert Moses turned this charming area into the Park's most enchanting fantasy landscape in the 1950s. Perhaps due to the popularity of E. B. White's immortal children's story *Stuart Little*, Moses was inspired to create a new Children's District—a child's version of Literary Walk on the Mall with the statues of *Alice in Wonderland* and *Hans Christian Andersen*. A statue of *Mary Poppins* was also offered, though it was not accepted.

Top: Ernest Lawson's painting Model Sailboat Pond, Central Park, New York *(c. 1904–07) captures the charm of this European-style area, originally intended to be the Park's formal garden.*

Bottom: Conservatory Water was designed to be the reflecting pool for a conservatory that was never built. The Model Boat Pond, as it is frequently called, has become New York's version of the Jardin du Luxembourg in Paris. The miniature yachts, once propelled by a strong wind and a long stick, now operate by remote control. The Central Park Yacht Club still holds regular regattas throughout the year.

Opposite: In the mid-nineteenth century formal gardens were planted in fanciful designs that resembled Oriental carpets. For an appreciation of such patterns, the viewer needed to look down at the garden from a high vantage point. For their competition entry, Olmsted and Vaux asked Jacob Wrey Mould to design such a garden for the site of the present Conservatory Water at Fifth Avenue and 74th Street, its steep embankment providing a perfect overlook.

The northeast corner of Central Park always featured important horticultural displays. The majestic trees of North America were a source of great national pride, and many entries to the design competition suggested that an arboretum be included in the Park. Olmsted and Vaux envisioned their arboretum for the entire northeast corner, which is now the site of the East Meadow, the Conservatory Garden, and the landscape that became the Harlem Meer.

When the funding fell through in 1871 for the proposed conservatory, the Park expanded the small garden and propagating house on the former site of Mount St. Vincent, directly above today's Conservatory Garden. At some point later in the century, a small nursery for growing plants for the Park was created on the site of the present garden.

The name Conservatory Garden was adopted in 1898 when a large E-shape greenhouse was constructed on Fifth Avenue and 105th Street. It featured an indoor winter garden of exotic tropical plants and decorative Victorian flower beds. In 1937, Commissioner Robert Moses hired the appropriately named landscape architect M. Betty Sprout to create the design and plantings for a new formal garden to replace the old greenhouse. The garden is divided into three separate areas, each one featuring a different style.

To Frederick Law Olmsted, pastoral and picturesque landscapes were the nourishment of the soul; architecture was dessert,

> as neither glass, nor china, nor knives and forks, nor even table and chairs are the essential elements of a dinner, so neither bridges, towers, shelters, seats, refectories, statues, cages for birds and animals, nor even drives and walks are the essential elements of the Park.[17]

Nonetheless the designers understood that the people needed structures for comfort, amenities for recreation, and sculpture for their cultural identity. The following two chapters on the architecture and sculpture of Central Park help us to understand those other elements that, combined with the landscapes, contribute to the Park's unique significance, both as a work of art and as a reflection of American history.

The northern display garden is in the geometric French style, featuring embroidered parterres and an ellipse of chrysanthemums in fall and tulips in spring.

The south garden was created in
the style of an English perennial
garden.

Above: Located on the East Meadow, the American elm, one of the Park's most magnificent horticultural features, may be the sole remaining tree from Olmsted and Vaux's plan to create an arboretum in the north end of the Park.

Opposite: The central Italianate garden of the Conservatory Garden features an expansive lawn, outlined by crab-apple allées that carpet the walkway with petals in springtime.

*The Frances Hodgson Burnett
Fountain and water-lily pool in
the south garden provide a
quiet retreat from the city as
well as a romantic backdrop
for many wedding ceremonies.
Dedicated to the author of the
children's classic* The Secret
Garden, *the fountain's two figures are often said to be those
of the main characters, Mary
and Dickon.*

America in the mid-nineteenth century was quite an interesting place for Calvert Vaux and Jacob Wrey Mould, two talented and ambitious architects from England. The nation was expanding rapidly, and good architects were in great demand. Because there were no architecture schools in the country, trained professionals had to be imported, which is why Andrew Jackson Downing had to travel to England to find himself a partner. In 1857 Vaux published *Villas and Cottages,* a pattern book that he had created for his clients, advertising a gamut of domestic structures, from villas for the wealthy to simple working-class cottages. In that same year Vaux and Mould, along with Richard Morris

Hunt, became founding members of the

nation's first professional architecture organ-

ization, the American Institute of Architects.

The opportunity to work in many new

styles was an exciting challenge at the time.

Americans of the eighteenth and early nine-

teenth centuries had equated their new

republic with ancient Greece and republican

Rome and, accordingly, had built classical

structures, such as the temple-fronted Federal

Hall on Wall Street. By the mid-nineteenth

century, global expansion had created a

passion for both historicism and exoticism.

The international exhibition held in 1853

at the Crystal Palace on Sixth Avenue and

42nd Street showcased objects and decorative arts designed in a cornucopia of styles: Moorish, Italian, Spanish, Egyptian, Gothic, Romanesque, Baroque, and rustic. Architects experimented with revival styles based on European examples. It was not long before the architecture of Central Park began to reflect the trends of the day.

Central Park fulfilled the cosmopolitan public's broadening appetite for foreign architecture and experiences. The Bandstand, a colorful Moorish structure by Jacob Wrey Mould, and the Venetian-style Mineral Springs Pavilion by Calvert Vaux brought Eastern exoticism to the heart of New York City. Mould's carvings, tiles, and proposed paving of Bethesda Terrace evoked both the Alhambra of Moorish Spain and the Gothic architecture of Venice, and Vaux's Belvedere Castle suggested a medieval Gothic Norman fortress. While the wealthy could afford to take the Grand Tour of Europe and the Near East, the middle and working classes were given a small taste of it in Central Park.

Opposite: Belvedere Castle against the backdrop of the New York City skyline.

Top: Central Park introduced New Yorkers to exotic animal species. The camel ride was led by a keeper dressed in Arabian costume.

Bottom: Nineteenth-century visitors could simulate a trip to Venice on a real gondola, given to the Park as a gift in 1862. Today a new gondola, The Bride of Venice, *provides the same experience.*

Anticipating the public's desire for a musical venue, the commissioners stipulated in the design competition that the Park include a music and exhibition hall. Initially Olmsted and Vaux placed their structure above the Mall, on the site of today's Rumsey Playfield. As the landscapes began to take shape, however, Olmsted envisioned a more transcendent presentation. Believing deeply that "landscape moves us in a manner more nearly analogous to the action of music than anything else," he orchestrated the fusion of

music to the scenery itself.[1] When the Ramble opened to the public in 1859, it was the site of the first concert. Visitors, positioned along the Lake, could hear the strains of the music waft over the water while enjoying the beautiful vista. Later, the musicians played from a boat in an attempt to have the music "float" across the water. Building on that venture, Olmsted suggested a "floating" bandstand across from the Terrace that could be positioned on an underground base in the Lake, while the audience would sit under the Terrace arcade.[2] The concept of combining water and music was finally put to rest in 1862 when Mayor George Opdyke transmitted a proposition to the board from Alfred Musard of Paris to erect a café that would also provide music "on the model of the 'Concert Musard' of Paris." The board voted in favor of the proposal (they probably had little choice), and later that year a cast-iron bandstand, somewhat suggestive of Musard's pavilion, appeared on dry ground.[3]

Just before descending the stairs to Mould's decorative Bethesda Terrace arcade, visitors would have passed his colorful Moorish-inspired jewel. The talented architect was also a lyricist and a translator of opera libretti, so it is only appropriate that he would create a structure that was music personified. His lyrics, "The Stars of Heav'n are Gleaming," were echoed in the designs on the Bandstand, a structure lined with a canopy of gilded stars on a sky-blue field. Decorated with symphony of colors and inscribed with the names of famous composers, it was the most fanciful attraction in the Park.

The Gazebo in Central Park *(1911)* by American painter *(Edward) Middleton Manigault captures the colorful effect of the original Bandstand and Mould's description of himself as "Hell on Color." A detailed account by Frederick Perkins describes Mould's polychrome layers from the bottom up: gray, bluish gray, olive green, red* brown, yellow, red and black, black, red, sky blue, gold, pea green and olive green, red, sky blue, gold, red brown, and green. The columns were bright red with gilt capitals; the rail-work of lotus flowers was white and gold, and the cupola featured bright gold stars in a dark blue field.

"You are what you drink" could have been the motto for nineteenth-century physicians and social reformers who recommended water for its healthful properties. "Taking the waters" was the panacea for all illnesses and considered to be the cure for alcoholism, so prevalent among the "dangerous classes," as poor immigrants were frequently called. Indeed, temperance advocates promoted Central Park as providing the antidote to this very real problem. A personification of that virtue was included as one of the allegorical cherubs on the Bethesda Fountain.

Above left: By 1867 the commissioners of the Park had given the firm of Schultz and Warker permission to set up a concession disbursing healthful mineral waters near the Green. Calvert Vaux designed the lavish Venetian Gothic fantasy to rival, perhaps, Mould's colorful and elaborate bandstand only steps away. The hexagonal counter, made of richly carved marble, was the central feature of an interior decorated with ornate tile and stenciling. Silver faucets dispensed artificial mineral waters concocted by Schultz's own recipe to replicate those from the world's most famous natural springs.

Above right: Vaux designed a two-story boathouse for the site where rowboats are presently rented. Old photographs reveal that the boats once had nature-inspired names such as Daisy, Violet, Rose, Lily, and Robin. Vaux's wooden building was replaced in the 1950s by a modern structure.

Landscape Follies

English tastemakers treated private estates as stage sets and frequently included "eye-catchers" or follies in their landscapes. These architectural fantasies helped draw visitors to prominent vistas or led them to surprising water sprays or the pretense of a scary cave or grotto. Follies were often ersatz "ruins," conjuring the exotic taste of ancient or distant cultures. Similarly, fanciful architecture was judiciously placed throughout Central Park to crown prominent outcrops, highlight an important view, and provide welcome shelter from the rain or sun on a hot summer day.

Rising out of Vista Rock, Belvedere Castle harmonizes perfectly with its site, as it was constructed from the same Manhattan schist as its natural perch. Built at three-quarter scale, the miniature castle provided the most arresting visual focus in the Park. The flag served as both a symbol of the nation and—according to Vaux—as "the culminating point of interest" from the Mall to Vista Rock. Affording views of the Park and the city, the tower is truly a *belvedere,* an architectural term for lookouts and observatories that literally means "beautiful view" in Italian.

Originally an open structure with no doors or windows, the Castle was weatherized in 1919 to accommodate the staff and meteorological instruments of the U.S. Weather Service, which transformed the medieval-style structure into year-round offices. The service stayed in the building until 1960, when weather began to be relayed electronically. Nonetheless, the instruments still record the official New York City weather via computer. We can flip the dial hourly to any radio station in New York and hear those famous words, "The weather in Central Park is . . . ." And because meteorologists are often the butt of jokes, it is somewhat appropriate that in New York City, at least, the weather comes to us directly from a folly.

Right: Originally Calvert Vaux designed a large castle and a smaller tower for the Belvedere complex; in 1871, during Vaux's absence from the Park project, a smaller pavilion, designed by Mould, was built to save costs. When Olmsted and Vaux returned the next year, they demolished the pavilion. The present structure is a modern reconstruction.

Opposite: Belvedere Castle, perched atop Vista Rock, was designed to evoke a medieval fortress such as those found throughout Europe. Until 1931, it overlooked the lower reservoir. Today the view is of the Great Lawn and Turtle Pond below.

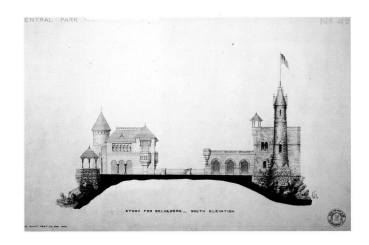

President Harry S. Truman called the War of 1812 "the silli-
est damn war we ever had," and why we fought it is a mystery to most Americans. If there is anything at all that we
remember, it is that the "bombs bursting in air" over a fort
in Baltimore Harbor prompted Francis Scott Key to write
the "Star Spangled Banner" poem. The blockhouse at
109th Street and Adam Clayton Powell Boulevard is the
last surviving fort on Manhattan Island from the war.

A string of blockhouses were constructed atop the rock
outcrops of Harlem Heights after New Yorkers became
threatened by a surprise attack on Long Island Sound at
Stonington, Connecticut, on August 27, 1814.[4] Until that
day, they had assumed that the British would attack from
the southern tip of the island, and they had built fortifications accordingly. Citizens from as far away as Brooklyn
and New Jersey hurriedly erected the protective fortifications in only one month.

Boats transported these workers daily from their distant
homes to the military sites. Many New Yorkers took advantage of these excursions not only to view the construction of
the forts but also to do some sightseeing. On September 20,
1814, the *New York Colombian* recommended to its readers
the beautiful landscapes made recently available to the
tourist: "The works at Harlem heights are numerous, com-
pact and judiciously placed, and form a romantic and
picturesque view." Fifty years later the land above 106th
Street became part of Central Park. At that time, the
Blockhouse was still viewed as a scenic ruin, its weathered
and crumbling stone walls draped with vines. Visitors
would be reminded of Ruskin's words that the "greatest
glory [of a building] is in its age."

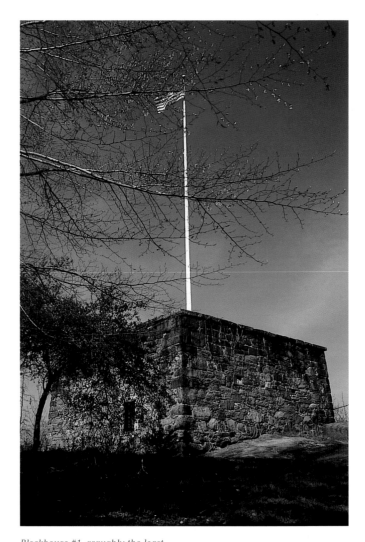

Blockhouse #1, arguably the least-
known structure in the Park, is the
only remaining fortification in the
area built for the War of 1812. It flies
the Stars and Stripes above a high
promontory from which American
troops could defend Manhattan
Island from possible attacks by
the British.

Though Central Park's Obelisk is an authentic Egyptian monument from c.1450 B.C., it resembled many of the ersatz ancient monuments created for eighteenth- and nineteenth-century European gardens.

New York, ever attempting to rival the capitals of Europe, had one reporter writing at the installation of the monument in 1881, "It would be absurd for the people of any great city to hope to be happy without the Egyptian Obelisk . . . . If New York was without one, all those great [cities] might point the finger of scorn at us and intimate that we could never rise to any real moral grandeur until we had our obelisk." And indeed, the monument was such an important symbol to Americans that President Rutherford B. Hayes even commented on its safe arrival in his final address to Congress.[5]

Calvert Vaux objected to the placement of the Obelisk in Central Park. Instead he thought it belonged in a major public square, as the great capitals of Europe all centered their obelisks in such prominent locations.[6] As recently as 1958, a letter to the *New York Times* suggested the Park's monument be moved to the new Lincoln Center plaza.[7] When artist, museum founder, and former Park commissioner Frederick Church suggested that the Obelisk be placed on Greywacke Knoll, the hill directly behind the Metropolitan Museum of Art, he was no doubt interested in the proximity of the ancient object to the new museum, as well as its relation to the lower reservoir. Church would have realized that the venerable Obelisk should flank the banks of a water body—in this case, the reservoir—a suggestion of its first location at Heliopolis on the Nile or its second one at Alexandria on the Mediterranean.

In the film The Ten Commandments, *Cecil B. DeMille included the scene of an obelisk-raising much like the one that occurred in Central Park in 1881, the year of his birth. In 1882 the board of commissioners forbade the sale of translations at the site of the Obelisk, but in 1956 the famous Hollywood director, who had grown up playing in the Park, gave the necessary funds for the translation plaque.*

Most historians will tell you that Cleopatra herself had nothing to do with her eponymous needle, having lived fifteen centuries after its erection. Her death occurred about twelve years before it was transported from Heliopolis to Alexandria with its twin, now on the banks of the Thames in London. Nonetheless, it was the Egyptian queen who had given orders for the obelisks to be moved to the Caesareum—the temple at Alexandria that Cleopatra built and dedicated to the memory of her lover, the deified Julius Caesar. About A.D. 18, in the reign of Augustus, the two columns were placed before the gates of the Caesareum.[8]

By the time the Romans reerected the obelisk at Alexandria, the four corners of the shaft were badly damaged. To steady the monument, the Romans placed four bronze crabs at the base of the shaft; two of the originals are in the Metropolitan Museum of Art, while the replicas in the Park are inscribed with the name of William Vanderbilt, who paid for the monument's long and arduous journey to America.[9]

Before its installation, a time capsule was buried under the Obelisk, the contents of which reveal much of what was important to Americans in 1880. Included among the items are the 1870 census, the Bible, *Webster's Dictionary,* the complete works of Shakespeare, a guide to Egypt, a facsimile of the Declaration of Independence, and a small box, the contents of which were known only to William Henry Hurlbert, who initiated the project.

The elegant Egyptian-style railing surrounding the monument was Jacob Wrey Mould's last creation for Central Park before he died in 1886.

Above: Most rustic shelters crowned prominent rock outcrops, adding a finishing touch to the landscape composition while also providing visitors with a welcome spot to rest. Copcot, Scottish for "head of a hill," overlooks the entire southern portion of the Park.

Opposite: The Park originally had many horticultural follies, including a maze and this Berceau Walk, both planted to hide the rectilinear reservoir walls.

By the 1750s, rustic work, constructed from unmilled branches, limbs, and roots of trees, arrived from China to decorate the picturesque landscapes on English estates. Andrew Jackson Downing, familiar with English examples, introduced his American clients and readers to rustic architecture; Vaux elaborated on this tradition. There were originally more than one hundred rustic summerhouses, pergolas, boat landings, fences, seats, signs, beehives, and birdhouses scattered throughout the Park.

Hungarian carpenter Anton Gerstner created most of the original rustic architecture in Central Park from Vaux's design specifications, such as this shelter in the Dene at 67th Street and Fifth Avenue.

The Kinderberg, whose name comes from the Dutch for "children's mountain," was designed by Vaux and situated on the crest of a rock outcrop across from the Dairy. At 110 feet in diameter, it was the largest and most elaborate rustic structure in the Park, and it featured rustic chairs and tables for children and their caregivers. Today it is the site of the brick Chess and Checkers House.

The character of rustic work, such as the roof in the Dene shelter, ultimately rests with the builder, who selects the twisted and gnarled branches that determine its style.

Not long after construction of the Park began, local newspapers criticized the plan for the lack of facilities for children and their caregivers. The board responded by requesting that the designers create a "children's department" in the lower part of the Park, convenient to the streetcars at 59th Street.[10] The features, grouped on the east and west sides of Playmates Arch included: the Dairy, an eatery and shelter; a Children's Cottage, a restroom and "petting zoo"; the Kinderberg, the largest rustic summerhouse in the Park; the Playground and Ballplayers' House, a ball field and changing room for boys; and, at a later date, the Carousel.

Girls were encouraged to take up croquet "as a fit substitute for base-ball." According to *Appleton's Journal*, the grounds were restricted to use by girls alone, "it being unwise to allow both sexes to play it together in so public a place." A croquet house was built on the present-day East Green near 69th Street and Fifth Avenue, and the sport continued there only until 1874, when it was considered too damaging to the lawn. As late as 1909 eighteen-year-old Ellen O'Connor defied police arrest in violating the rule that still limited ball playing to boys under sixteen.

The Children's District also included a playground, a nineteenth-century term for a lawn meant for sports such as cricket and the newly emerging game of "base-ball," though the game was restricted to boys only. The Ballplayers' House, a changing room for the players, was designed by Calvert Vaux. It was demolished in the 1960s and replaced in 1991 by a refreshment stand that evokes the charm of the old building.

Set on an outcrop just below the Kinderberg, the Children's Cottage was designed to resemble a country farmhouse. Upstairs was a rest room, a dressing room, and a counter from which children could get games and toys to play with in the adjacent Kinderberg. A stable planned for the lower level was intended to feature "a cow or two, a ewe with lambs and a few broods of chickens," as Olmsted and Vaux felt that urban children should experience the rapidly disappearing rural life. However, the Tweed administration turned the building into a paint shed. Sometime before the turn of the century, it was demolished.

Built between 1869 and 1871, the Dairy is one of Central Park's most picturesque structures. English landscape designer Humphrey Repton noted in the late eighteenth century that estate dairies were always designed in the Gothic style, and Vaux's jewel-like structure follows that tradition.[11] Vaux designed the charming structure in the same manner as the contemporary cottages he was creating for his private suburban clients. The Gothic Revival style is characterized by steep, pointed gables and gingerbread bargeboards that echo Gothic tracery. The loggia, always an important element of Downing and Vaux's domestic architecture, is prominent at the Dairy. In times without air-conditioning or electric fans, the breezes from the Pond to the south provided welcome relief to visitors, many of whom lived downtown in crowded and unventilated tenements.

The Dairy was nearing completion in April 1870 when a new city charter affected the Park's development and its management for the next nineteen months. Power in the city shifted from the old state legislature-appointed administration to the newly created municipal government, headed by the charismatic and corrupt William Marcy "Boss" Tweed, self-appointed Commissioner of Public Works, and his Ring of underhanded and inept Tammany Hall cronies. The crooked Peter "Brains" Sweeney and the notorious Judge Henry Hilton headed the new five-man Department of Public Parks. The incorruptible Andrew Haswell Green was retained by the new board but was stripped of any real power. Thomas Fields, the Democratic commissioner who had tried in 1858 to block the Greensward plan from being considered for the competition, remained in his post.[12] And coming out of retirement, Olmsted and Vaux's old nemesis, Robert J. Dillon, once again held the reins of power.[13]

The Dairy, built in 1869–71. Today it is one of the Park's visitor centers.

Dillon's long-held desire for a straight and wide carriage drive was realized at last. The 1871 *First Annual Report of the Department of Public Parks* proudly reported that many of the "hitherto constricted and dangerous portions" of the roads were straightened as much as possible. Olmsted and Vaux's curves were softened on the East Drive, and the road was widened in parts twelve additional feet—"a great relief to those visiting the Park in carriages." Both of these "improvements" finally provided carriage drivers with the opportunity for racing that Dillon and Belmont had fought for thirteen years earlier.[14]

The new board made other changes to the landscape that were diametrically opposed to the aesthetics of Olmsted and Vaux. Dillon, like Richard Morris Hunt, had always preferred that the Park be integrated with the urban landscape by continuing the straight avenues of the city into a Parisian-style park of open vistas and formal plantings. Many walks in the Park were straightened. Trees that had screened out the city were either transplanted elsewhere—often to other city parks—or stripped of their lower branches until, as the *New York Times* later remarked, they looked like "telephone poles." Tweed philosophy reasoned that residents along the perimeter deserved open views into the landscape, as they were assessed at a higher tax rate. Conversely, the new board felt that visitors in the Park would enjoy views out to the luxurious mansions in the same way they enjoyed looking at the afternoon carriage parade.

The new board swept away fifteen years of Olmsted and Pilat's picturesque plantings, viewing them as "an undergrowth of cat-briers and tangled weeds." Luxurious vines that the men had lovingly trained to grow over the ornamental bridges were removed. Any artful plantings that prevented those in carriages or on horseback from having broad, open vistas were unearthed and left for the compost heap. The site of the Dairy, which was intended to be in a secluded location, had its paths straightened and shrubbery removed. The quiet retreat for children and invalids became instead a popular eatery, a feature that lasted well into the 1950s.

The most sweeping change to the Park envisioned by Olmsted and Vaux was not in the landscape but in the massive building program that emphasized the prominence of structures and the importance of popular amusements, educational institutions, and new amenities for Park visitors. The new board retained Jacob Wrey Mould and promoted him to Olmsted's former title of architect-in-chief. Mould immediately went to work fulfilling the requests of the new administration, from major buildings to badges for Park police to an iron settee, which Commissioner Dillon had brought from Paris and instructed Mould to copy.

The loveliest legacy of the Tweed administration is Jacob Wrey Mould's elegant "ombra," or shaded pavilion, built for visitors waiting for a carriage ride into the Park. Originally there was such a pavilion on each corner of 59th Street. When the Maine Memorial was installed on Columbus Circle in 1913, the decorative structure was moved to Hernshead, a promontory on the west side of the Lake. Now known as Ladies' Pavilion, it probably takes its unofficial name from either its proximity to the former Ladies' Pond or from Victorian etiquette, for a proper lady never exposed herself directly to the sun.

Manhattan's private pleasure grounds featured merry-go-rounds or "flying horses," as they were more often called. The new Tweed board, preferring to amuse and entertain the public rather than elevate its morals through landscape design, installed a carousel in the children's district. The earliest guidebooks mention a "circular building containing a large number of hobby-horses, which move around a large circle by means of machinery," revealed by one unidentified pamphlet as a hand crank.

Turning the merry-go-round day after day must have made someone . . . well, very cranky, and in 1873 the solution to the problem became a new feature unto itself. After the demise of the Tweed administration, Olmsted and Vaux moved the building fifty feet north so that a basement with access to the transverse road could be constructed. The new machinery—a horse hitched to the lower part of the center pole—was more amusing to children than the ride itself. Boys and girls loved to lie flat on the ground to get a peek of the horse—some accounts say "mule"—through the basement windows. In response to two taps on the floor, the animal would start; one tap, and he would stop.[15] As recently as 1912, a horse was still on the treadmill, but a few years later "horse power" gave way to electricity, and about 1924 the third carousel, with metal horses and a brass ring, was installed.

On November 8, 1950, New Yorkers awakened to the sad news that the Central Park Carousel had burned to the ground. A replacement was soon found in an old trolley terminal at Coney Island. At the turn of the century, entrepreneurial trolley companies built small amusement parks with food concessions and picnic tables at the end of the line in order to attract ridership. When the trolley line was discontinued, the carousel was put into storage. Fortunately, the abandoned attraction just so happened to be a masterpiece of American folk art by the Rembrandts of carousel artistry, Sol Stein and Harry Goldstein.

Russian immigrants Stein and Goldstein, former carvers of women's combs, emigrated to Williamsburg, Brooklyn, when the burgeoning art form of carousel making was at its height, and founded the Artistic Carroussel Manufacturing Company. Their flamboyant horses had trademark features, most of which can be seen on the Central Park Carousel: bulging glass eyes, big teeth, fish-scale armor, and manes and tails appearing to blow from the forward motion. The outer horses were always twice as large as those on the inner circle. There were two chariots on every ride, flaunting the company's signature ornamentation of deeply carved cabbage roses. Carved inner and outer panels of the ride are unique to Stein and Goldstein.[16]

Opposite: The first carousel in Central Park was powered by a hand crank. A few years later manpower was replaced by horsepower—a real horse that was harnessed to a pole on the lower level of the structure.

This page: The present carousel was originally designed for Coney Island. Considered a masterpiece of American folk art, it was moved to the site after the previous structure burned in 1950.

The Institutions

Olmsted and Vaux did not promote Central Park as a civic center featuring cultural, artistic, and scientific institutions. Nonetheless, other civic leaders and commissioners—particularly Andrew Haswell Green—felt that scientific institutions, in particular, made a city "the acknowledged seat of wealth and moral power," and they encouraged their incorporation into the Park.[17] Green pushed for the establishment of a menagerie, the Museum of Natural History, the Paleozoic Museum, the New-York Historical Society, an astronomical observatory, and a weather station.

Completed in 1851 and built as a storage facility for munitions, the Arsenal became office space for the Park administrators. When gifts poured in from around the world to the new Park—paintings and sculptures, weaponry, various artifacts, and specimens of natural history—the Arsenal became the Park's first museum. The American Museum of Natural History opened in the basement of the Arsenal in 1871. The exhibits remained there until 1877, when a new building, designed by Vaux and Mould, opened to the public at the present Manhattan Square site, which had been formerly chosen by Olmsted and Vaux for the Menagerie.

THE MENAGERIE

Above: Some of the animals given as gifts to the new Park were tethered to poles on the grounds outside the Arsenal. For a brief period of time, live animals were even kept in the basement. The Menagerie buildings were designed by Jacob Wrey Mould.

Opposite: The Arsenal, built in 1851 for munitions storage, served as the Park's first museum building. The building also housed meteorologist Dr. Daniel Draper's weather observatory, which was open to the public.

The Park began to receive animals as gifts in the 1860s, and the commissioners realized that they had to establish a zoological garden or menagerie. In 1871, the Tweed administration ordered Jacob Wrey Mould to design temporary structures on the Arsenal grounds, with the intention to move an enlarged menagerie to the upper Park once construction was complete. By the time the former commissioners returned to power in November 1871, a deer house had already been completed on the North Meadow; Olmsted and Vaux ordered it to be demolished.

Although animals have been on the site of the Zoo since the Park began, a permanent facility was not established until 1934, under Commissioner Robert Moses. The current Zoo, designed by Kevin Roche, John Dinkeloo & Associates, was opened in 1988. It has always been one of the Park's most popular features.

Above: Because of their Darwinian link to humans, monkeys, more than any other zoo animal, fascinated and often repelled nineteenth-century visitors. The present Zoo features playful animals such as these snow monkeys.

Opposite: Most people mistakenly think that the American Museum of Natural History was the first institution intended to feature a dinosaur display in New York City. Surprisingly, however, the first Paleozoic Museum, a separate institution, was planned for a site just inside the Park at Central Park West and 63rd Street. British sculptor Benjamin Waterhouse Hawkins was creating models of the extinct animals in a studio on the grounds of the Arsenal when vandals destroyed his work in 1871.

In fall 1858, workmen in Haddonfield, New Jersey, uncovered a Hadrosaurus, the first-known, complete skeleton of a dinosaur on the North American continent. Exactly ten years later the board of commissioners hired British sculptor and artist Benjamin Waterhouse Hawkins to create a model of that Hadrosaurus and other "pre-Adamite creatures" or "monsters"—as they are still called in England today—for a new museum.

Commissioner Green asked the British sculptor to re-create life-size dinosaurs as he had done for the Crystal Palace Park in Sydenham, England, in 1854. Working with British paleontologist Sir Richard Owen—who had coined the term *dinosaur* (Greek for "awesome lizard")—the two men attempted the first life-size dinosaur reconstruction in history.

In 1869 Hawkins set up a studio somewhere near the Arsenal and began construction of his models. By spring 1870 he had completed his thirty-nine-foot Hadrosaurus and two of the other twelve planned models of extinct animals, but the new Tweed administration discontinued his project. Though the Tweed board professed merit in the new though "imperfect" science and even considered pairing the project with an aquarium, ultimately they chose to enlarge the Zoo, giving priority to live animals over extinct ones.

Their benign but dismissive attitude toward dinosaurs and paleontology was not commensurate with the violent act of May 3, 1871, when henchmen, acting on the order of Tweed-appointed Park Commissioner Henry Hilton, entered Hawkins's studio with sledgehammers, destroyed the enormous concrete-and-iron models, and carted the fragments almost two and a half miles away to be buried at the grounds of Mount St. Vincent.

One can only guess that the remote burial site was a response to Hawkins's attempt to establish a private museum that would rival the thwarted public one that was to be established on the Mount St. Vincent site. On March 6, just three months before the vandalism occurred, leading artists, scientists, and civic leaders of the influential Lyceum of Natural History—Commissioner Green included—listened to the troubled sculptor plead for support of a Paleozoic Museum for the Park. The meeting became rather heated when critics of the Tweed government openly expressed opinions on their corruption. In the process a speaker revealed the sculptor's secret agenda to create a museum in the city "without a corresponding scheme for dividing the profits." In true entrepreneurial spirit, the artist had tried in vain to circumvent the Tweed Ring's cancellation of the project and strike out on his own.[18]

With smashed models and broken dreams, Hawkins spent many more years trying to realize his vision. The sculptor sued the commissioners for more than $16,000 in back pay, compensation for his materials, and the breach of contract, but restitution never came. The entrepreneurial Hawkins created several small, saleable models of the dinosaurs, which gave birth to the contemporary phenomenon of dinomania. The only reminders we have of what might have been in Central Park are the dinosaurs that still survive in Crystal Palace Park in Bromley, a quiet suburb of London.

Just two months after Hawkins's creatures came to their violent demise, the corruption and greed of the Tweed administration were exposed in the *New York Times*. By November 1872, the Park was once again in the hands of the former board of commissioners. Olmsted and Vaux were reinstated to their old positions as landscape architects.

Before creating his iron and concrete dinosaur models for Central Park, Hawkins spent six months traveling through North America to learn about the continent's extinct animals. He is credited with reconstructing the first dinosaur skeleton, the Hadrosaurus, shown here and presented to the Academy of Natural Sciences in Philadelphia.

More than 1600 people lived and worked on the land that became Central Park. One of the largest communities was the Sisters of Charity of Mount St. Vincent, a Catholic convent and school for more than two hundred nuns and girls situated on a hill above Fifth Avenue and 105th Street.

After the order relocated to a new home in the Bronx, both the Olmsted and Vaux families lived in the building complex during the first years of the Park's construction. From 1862 to 1865 the buildings were used as a hospital for Union soldiers, and the Sisters returned to nurse them. After the Civil War, the collection of art and natural history objects was moved to the former convent from the Arsenal, and the buildings became the Park's new restaurant, museum, and display garden. They burned down in 1881.

Two years later the Mount St. Vincent restaurant was constructed on the site. When the Sisters of Charity complained that their name was being used for an establishment associated with drinking, rowdy behavior, and Tammany Hall politicians, the name was changed to McGowan's Pass Tavern. The building was torn down by anti-Tammany officials around 1915. Today the land is the composting area of the Park.[19]

The chapel building of Mount St. Vincent, the convent and school that predated Central Park, photographed from the shore of the Harlem Meer.

Mount St. Vincent became Manhattan's first uptown museum. The Chapel of the Immaculate Conception was converted into a gallery featuring the work of the American sculptor Thomas Crawford, whose statue Freedom adorns the dome of the Capitol in Washington, D.C. Crawford was America's foremost neoclassical sculptor in the 1850s. After his untimely death in 1857, Crawford's widow, Louisa, promised to donate the collection of her husband's plaster casts to any American institution that would pay the cost of shipping them from Rome. The Central Park board of commissioners obviously saw the offer as an opportunity to obtain an instant art collection for the Park. An assortment of art objects, specimens of natural history, and military items, given as gifts to the Park, were displayed on the lower floor.

THE METROPOLITAN MUSEUM OF ART

In the Greensward plan, the site of the Metropolitan Museum of Art was intended to be one of the three playgrounds; but when a flock of deer was given as a gift, it became a deer park. In 1872 the board of the downtown museum accepted the present site, though it considered the remoteness of the location a detriment to the success of the museum.[20] The first building, designed in the Ruskinian Gothic style by Vaux and Mould and erected in 1880, has been subsumed by later additions.

Olmsted and Vaux were founding members of the Metropolitan Museum of Art. Later additions surrounded Vaux and Mould's original 1880 building, the west facade of which is visible within the Lehman Wing.

THE SHEEPFOLD

In the 1860s, Central Park's sheep were housed in temporary sheds and packed into confined spaces with no light and poor ventilation, causing the loss of several animals. Before they were ousted by the Tweed administration, Olmsted and Vaux planned for a barn and stable on the transverse road at 86th Street. The new board, however, felt that commuting twenty blocks to work was too much for the animals, and they authorized Mould to create housing adjacent to the meadow. The structure was intended to also feature an exhibition space on sheep husbandry and products.

When Olmsted and Vaux were reinstated as landscape architects, soon after the sheep and their keeper had moved in, they were horrified at the enormity of the building and its prominent placement on the meadow.[21] Nonetheless, the Ruskinian Gothic building housed the sheep and the shepherd until 1934, when Robert Moses removed the flock and transformed the building into the world-famous Tavern on the Green restaurant.

Original granite, brick, and Minton tile details of Mould's 1871 Sheepfold can still be seen on the facade of the building, now the Tavern on the Green restaurant.

THE SKYLINE

In 1857, as Olmsted and Vaux were creating the Greensward plan, Elisha Otis designed and installed the first passenger elevator in a New York City building. Innocently, the Park's designers had thought that an artful and judicious placement of "verdure" could screen out the encroaching five- and six-story buildings.[22] Though Olmsted predicted that the Park would eventually "be surrounded by an artificial wall, twice as high as the Great Wall of China, composed of urban buildings," he could never have predicted the ascendancy of the skyscraper, which no arrangement of trees could ever camouflage.

The famous New York skyline frames the equally famous work of landscape art.

In the nineteenth century, Easterners, accustomed to smooth, verdant mountaintops, were appalled at the first photographs of the jagged and treeless Rocky Mountains. Similarly, the next generation was unsettled by the irregular New York skyline. Writing in 1928, Frederick Law Olmsted Jr. lamented the skyline's damage to his father's urban retreat, abhorring not only the "crude and ugly restlessness of the ill-composed skylines," but also its "inharmonious" background to the landscape.[23] Today we have a much broader definition of beauty and embrace the uneven horizons of both mountains and skyscrapers. We celebrate Central Park as New York's magnificent landscape painting and do not separate it from its equally celebrated and awesome picture frame.

CHAPTER 6: THE SCULPTURE

The designers of Central Park were not in favor of placing sculpture in the landscapes or even around the perimeter of the Park. With the exception of Bethesda Terrace, they wanted the Park to be free of "incidents," as Olmsted termed sculpture and other nonlandscape features. By 1866 only two statues had been erected and a few more proposed, yet the distressed Olmsted criticized the Park for having "too much incident" and anticipated that "the worst" was yet to come.[1] Very early on, however, it was clear that the Park was a new democratic institution to be shaped and defined by the public.

The sculptures and monuments have played a central role in that process and contribute to the Park's status as a complex work of art.

The Park's collection of sculpture represents the most important artists and stylistic movements of nineteenth- and twentieth-century America. Neoclassicism, realism, Beaux-Arts monumentality, folk art, modernism, and conceptual art are all represented in Central Park, as well as the breadth of American history from the Civil War to the Cold War, and a range of cultural figures from Beethoven to John Lennon and from the Ugly Duckling to Mother Goose.

The Sculptures in Context

When the Park began to receive gifts of sculpture, the designers decided to place many of them symmetrically in line with the stately elms on the Mall, the Park's most formal landscape. The statues of *Shakespeare* and *Columbus* at the southern end of the Mall adhere to this concept. They are literally the same size and figuratively of equally historic stature. By the time that we arrive at the statues of *Sir Walter Scott* and *Robert Burns,* we expect the sculptures to be presented in pairs: in this case, two seated figures, two writers, two Scotsmen.

The company that a sculpture keeps—an important element of siting—gives significant meaning to the work itself. So arriving at the next figure, *Fitz-Greene Halleck* by James Wilson Alexander McDonald (1876), we are thrown off balance; the sculpture is alone, no other figure sits across from it. And then there's the man himself, Fitz-Greene Halleck. Who was he? He has pen and paper in hand and a messy pile of books under his chair, so we can surmise that he belongs on Literary Walk—an unofficial name for the southern section of the Mall—but the other sculpted figures are so well known by comparison.

How can we appreciate these works without judging them by our current standards of taste or by our lack of familiarity with the subject? Halleck, for example, was actually a well-known poet and social wit of his day and—whether we like the statue or not—we can at least appreciate it as a monument to poetry, an art form that was highly valued at the time. When the sculpture was unveiled in 1877, ten years after the poet's death, more than ten thousand people crowded into Central Park to watch the President of the United States, Rutherford B. Hayes, and his cabinet present the sculpture to the city.

The commissioners of the Park, recognizing the phenomenon of fleeting fame, were concerned about littering the landscape with monuments to less-than-significant figures. In 1873, Calvert Vaux, artist and commissioner Frederick Church, and Park board president Henry Stebbins suggested some guidelines for the future.[2] First, they proposed that a person be dead at least five years before he or

Opposite: The south end of the Mall is unofficially known as Literary Walk due to the many sculptures of writers that line the pathway.

Above: Fitz-Greene Halleck, the only American poet on Literary Walk, is the least-known figure today. He was quite a popular poet and social wit in the nineteenth century.

she could be so memorialized. Halleck obviously passed the test, as he was still very popular ten years after his death in 1867—it is only 110 years after his death that he has been forgotten.

To address the issue of aesthetics, the committee stipulated that judgment as to the "merits as a work of art" shall pass the approval of professional art institutions and associations, and that "the determination of a site for any statue shall be reserved until after its acceptance." Authority in evaluating artistic quality and merit was eventually legislated into existence by the establishment of the Art Commission in 1898, a governmental arm of the City of New York that, along with the New York City Landmarks Preservation Commission and the local community boards, reviews all sculpture proposals for Central Park today.

Legislation, however, can never arbitrate style and taste. Over the years several sculptures have been removed from the Park. Even *Shakespeare,* so synonymous today with the Mall, was once considered unworthy of a place in Central Park.[3] No one in the nineteenth century complained about MacDonald's *Halleck.* The work reflected contemporary fashion—the way the men wore their whiskers, how they dressed, the kind of chairs they had. Halleck is typical of the Victorian gentleman who would have been seen promenading down the Mall in 1877. We can appreciate his statue as a work of art of the Victorian era.

If we rely only on our current standard of taste, we lose an opportunity to have an important dialogue with the past. In this chapter, we will trace the evolution of sculpture in Central Park and examine the ways in which the works function within their historical and physical contexts.

Icons and Heroes

INDIAN HUNTER

The young American John Quincy Adams Ward (named after the sixth president), who created *Indian Hunter* (placed in 1869) and *Shakespeare* (placed in 1872), was celebrated for replacing the old European Neoclassical tradition with Realism, the first truly American school of sculpture. Ward was the first American sculptor to train at home, having apprenticed with Henry Kirke Brown, a noted American who had studied in Rome.

American painters of the mid-nineteenth century were searching for their authentic voice—a voice some found by depicting genre scenes and others by portraying the wildness of the American landscape. So too a new generation of sculptors chose to create models of the nation's indigenous peoples. When Ward's almost-life-size *Indian Hunter* was first exhibited in 1865 in a New York art gallery, critics celebrated the work, claiming it "so entirely American" that it "will vindicate American art and evidence . . . American genius."[4]

In 1860, Ward had originally created the *Indian Hunter* as a small bronze statuette that followed the longstanding tradition of representing Native Americans with idealized European features, particularly those found on classical

Before creating the Central Park Indian Hunter, *Ward originally sculpted a small bronze statuette with classical features, following in the artistic tradition of likening Native Americans to ancient Greeks and Romans.*

Greek or Roman statues.[5] Committed to creating art from a direct experience with nature, Ward journeyed to the Dakotas to study Native-American culture and, as a result, he transformed the small statuette into a larger and more heroic figure whose physiognomy, hair, and clothing—incised with a subtle tribal pictograph—represented a more authentic image. Critics celebrated the image as "a great refreshment after our plumed, bald-headed, Roman-nosed . . . Indian of English poetry, of bank notes, school orations and the stage."[6]

Native-American people held a deep, personal significance for the young Quincy Ward. The artist's great-uncle John, his grandfather's brother, was captured as a child in 1758 by the Shawnee tribe and raised as a member of it until his death. Many years after the abduction, hunter Simon Kenton, a friend of the artist's grandfather, was taken prisoner by the same tribe. Kenton met John, who remembered his family name and claimed that he often tried unsuccessfully to visit them. John was killed when he tried to leave the tribe to find the Wards and to establish harmony between the two races. The artist's grandfather found his brother's Shawnee wife and children and attempted to maintain ties with them for the rest of his life—a situation, no doubt, that sensitized the sculptor to the depiction of indigenous peoples. The artist's two versions of the *Indian Hunter*—one with European features and one with Native-American features—might also reflect an ambivalence toward his lost relative and the tribe that captured him.[7] The *Indian Hunter* was the most personally satisfying work of the artist's life, and Ward requested that a copy of it mark his own grave in Urbana, Ohio.

Above: Indian Hunter *(1865), by John Quincy Adams Ward, was celebrated for combining Neoclassicism with the emerging Realism and the new attention to American subjects.*

John Quincy Adams Ward's
Shakespeare, *created in 1870*
and placed in the park two
years later, reflects the popular-
ity of the Bard in nineteenth-
century America. Steele McKay,
an actor and friend of the artist,
suggested the contemplative
pose. America's most famous
Shakespearean actor, Edwin
Booth, offered Ward Elizabethan
costumes and invited him to
performances as to better pre-
pare him for an authentic
representation of the dramatist.

In nineteenth-century America people at every level of society knew their Shakespeare. It was fitting, therefore, that this venerated populist figure be represented by a prominent monument in America's quintessentially democratic space.

Americans were determined to adopt Europe's most notable genius as their own countryman. At the statue's dedication in May 1872, keynote speaker William Cullen Bryant likened the Bard to both the venerable redwood groves in the West and to Niagara Falls, considered the most majestic of American landscapes. A poem, briefly fastened to the temporary base of the monument, staked a claim to the Bard's American birthright, "Old World, he is not only thine/Our New World too has a part/As opulent and divine/In his stupendous mind and heart."[8]

Shakespeare's "stupendous mind" was considered the most valued feature of the man. The locus of his greatness—his head and brain—was the most significant feature of Ward's likeness. Bryant, like many of his contemporaries, believed in phrenology, the popular nineteenth-century pseudoscience that explained an individual's character, morality, and intelligence by the shape and size of his or her skull. In his speech, he invoked the expertise of "phrenologists of the present day [who] . . . tell you of the visible indications of his boundless invention."[9] Only a year before Ward started to model the statue, *Coombs' Popular Phrenology*, published in 1865, illustrated Shakespeare's broad and high forehead, his immense head, and his balding pate exemplifying his genius.[10]

Although the term *highbrow* did not come into the vernacular until the 1880s and its converse, *lowbrow,* until the turn of the century, most late-nineteenth-century visitors to Central Park were accustomed to "reading" sculptures with a phrenological interpretation.[11] Just as most newspaper accounts praised Ward's *Shakespeare* for its close approximation to the poet's real head, so too did they admire the head of *Indian Hunter* for its realistic treatment of a Native American, although the Indian's low brow implied an inferior mental and moral condition to the superior Northern European, Anglo-Saxon skull exhibited on Shakespeare.[12] Ward's two sculptures, placed in close proximity, thus confirmed for Park visitors the "proof" of one's biological destiny, as they believed it to be.

Above left: The decades after the Civil War were a time of healing, and Daniel Webster, *dedicated in 1876 for the country's centennial anniversary, represents the decision by civic leaders to celebrate the democratic foundation of the Union through a monument to the nation's grandest and most eloquent figure of his time.*

Above right: The Pilgrim by John Quincy Adams Ward, dedicated in 1885, stands on a knoll overlooking the East Drive at 72nd Street, subtly encouraging us to share in his westward view of Central Park. Coincidentally, the statue also looks across the 72nd Street Drive toward the monument of Daniel Webster, whose 1820 Plymouth oration shaped the image of the pilgrim as an American icon.

DANIEL WEBSTER

In order to understand the legendary status Daniel Webster enjoyed in his lifetime and for many years after his death, it is useful to find a modern equivalent. The most powerful and effective orator of our time was arguably Dr. Martin Luther King, and Massachusetts Senator Daniel Webster was Dr. King's nineteenth-century American counterpart. Charismatic, magnetic, and forceful speakers, both Webster and King had dreams of national unity and harmony. They both earned their reputations in a sorely divided country— one during the years of slavery, the other during the emerging Civil Rights movement. Unlike Dr. King, Webster was invited and expected to speak at all important national occasions. He was so popular that thousands of middle-class homes had two-foot-high bronze statuettes of Webster by Thomas Ball in their living rooms.

Webster was the personification of monumentality itself; *giant* and *Olympian* were terms frequently used to describe him. After his famous 1843 oration for the dedication of the Bunker Hill Monument, a reporter for the New York *Herald* wrote, "It was a scene of singular sublimity. The tall pillar in all its impressive solemnity . . . the majestic figure of the orator as he stood silently regarding the colossal column . . . all made up a scene never to be forgotten."[13] Ralph Waldo Emerson, also present, summed it up succinctly: "There was the Monument, and here was Webster."[14] So when donor Gordon Webster Burnham—a namesake of the orator—wanted to enlarge Ball's statuette into a thirty-four-foot-high monument, no one thought the size out of proportion to the man's reputation.

Olmsted and Vaux opposed Burnham's intended site for the colossus—the oval bed at the south end of the Mall.

Burnham's site was a reasonable request, adhering to a Park rule that cited the Mall as a place reserved for the sculptures of such prominent figures.[15] But the statue would have dwarfed the other sculptures and completely disturbed the scale and design of the most important landscape in the Park. The designers forcefully intervened. In their letter to the board, they also objected to the proposed site where *Webster* stands today—the junction of the West Drive at 72nd Street, "the busiest and most disturbed place in all the Park."[16] At this site the back of the statue is as prominent as the front, a feature that both Olmsted and Vaux found objectionable. Nonetheless, in the early 1850s—when the memory of the living man was still fresh in the minds of the public—the body of the orator was so familiar and so legendary that he was identifiable from every vantage point.[17]

Carl Conrads's staid statue of Alexander Hamilton, a founding father of the United States, memorializes a fascinating episode of early New York history and a poignant personal story as well. When the statue was placed in 1880, it would have flanked the old Croton Reservoir, a triumph of technology over the fears of disease and fire. Nearly a century earlier, Hamilton was intricately involved in trying to develop a water system for the city. Surprisingly, he backed a plan that was hatched by his archenemy Aaron Burr, the man who would mortally wound him in a duel in 1804. The plan ultimately failed, and thirty years after Hamilton's death the city still lacked an adequate water supply.

The worst of these fears was realized on December 17, 1835, when New York experienced the most destructive fire in its young history. It began in warehouses along Pearl Street. Water from the city's small reservoir had been depleted by two previous fires that day, so when the flames reached Wall Street, the only way to contain the blaze was to blow up several buildings in hopes of creating a fireproof void. Valiantly, Hamilton's son James initiated the explosion of 48 Merchant's Place in an attempt to save the neighboring Merchant's Exchange Building. James Hamilton knew the building contained a marble effigy of his father and he watched helplessly as a few brave men tried in vain to save it before the roof collapsed upon it.

For forty-five years, James Hamilton lived with the memory of the fire and the destruction of his father's memorial. In 1880 he rectified the situation by commissioning the Central Park sculpture. Placed beside the newly erected Obelisk—itself a symbol of permanence and endurance—*Hamilton* was sited near the juncture of the two reservoirs. Whereas the original sculpture had been carved of soft marble—believed to be the first marble sculpture carved in the United States—Central Park's monument is of a durable and fireproof granite.[18]

Alexander Hamilton *(1880), placed in Central Park by his son James Hamilton, memorializes a poignant personal story.*

Danish-born Albert Bertel Thorvaldsen was the leading European sculptor of his time, succeeding the more recognized Antonio Canova. This slightly less-than-life-size self-portrait, donated by Danish-American citizens, is an 1892 bronze copy of an 1839 original marble in Copenhagen. It occupies the most obscure site in Central Park—a traffic island between the East 96th and 97th Street transverse roads.[19]

The work is a sculpture of a sculptor sculpting his sculpture. Thorvaldsen, who produced the piece when he was almost seventy years old, depicted himself as a young, idealized Greek god, chisel and mallet in hand, leaning on a diminutive version of his statue, *Hope*.

Before the nineteenth century there were no renowned American sculptors; aspiring, young Americans emigrated to Rome to study with masters such as Thorvaldsen. The predominant style of the day was Neoclassicism or "the correct style," a conscious imitation of ancient Greek and Roman idealized forms, of which Thorvaldsen's self-portrait is a typical example. American Emma Stebbins, who created the Park's most famous Neoclassical work, the *Angel of the Waters* fountain at Bethesda Terrace, also studied and worked in Rome. By the time Stebbins's angel was dedicated in 1873, however, it was considered out of style, and one can imagine that *Thorvaldsen*, being a copy of an earlier work, must have seemed somewhat anachronistic in 1892.

Albert Bertel Thorvaldsen, *a self-portrait of the prominent Danish sculptor, is an 1892 bronze copy of an 1839 original marble in Copenhagen.*

The famous architect Richard Morris Hunt died in 1895 at age sixty-seven while he was in the midst of working on his additions to the Metropolitan Museum of Art. In his honor the Architectural League of New York recommended constructing the 59th Street gates, the same project that had been the undoing of Calvert Vaux. Instead, however, the Municipal Art Society—Hunt had been its founding president—organized a fund-raising drive and hired Hunt's student architect Bruce Price and sculptor Daniel Chester French to fashion a grand monument to Hunt's memory across from his most famous New York building, the Lenox Library (now the site of the Frick Museum).

The semicircular memorial is in the classical Beaux-Arts style. It features a bench below a series of Ionic columns and bronze allegories of the visual arts: "Painting and Sculpture" is represented by a classically draped female holding a palette in one hand and a mallet and miniature Dionysus from the Parthenon in the other; "Architecture" holds a model of Hunt's Administration Building for the 1893 World's Colombian Exposition in Chicago. In the center is a pleasant portrait bust of the dapper Hunt, who, by most accounts, "wasn't a pleasant person."[20] The allegories to the visual arts are not only references to the fields in which Hunt was involved, but also a nod to both his proposed program for the Artists' Gate and the proposed allegorical figures of the four arts that were intended for Hunt's new facade of the Metropolitan Museum of Art. In the 1960s both female statues were stolen from the monument and then retrieved from a factory just before they were about to be melted down to make belt buckles.[21]

In New York only Hunt's additions to the Metropolitan Museum of Art and the base of the Statue of Liberty remain as examples of his major works. His legacy includes the founding of the eleven professional art institutions inscribed on the monument. Throughout his lifetime, Hunt also generously nurtured and promoted the work of young sculptors and architects, such as French and Price, the creators of his memorial, and Augustus Saint-Gaudens, the incomparable sculptor of the monument to General William Tecumseh Sherman.

The Richard Morris Hunt Memorial once faced the Lenox Library, one of architect's most famous buildings (formerly on the site of the Frick Museum). A bust of Hunt is shown between female personifications of Painting and Sculpture, who holds a palette and a miniature sculpture from the Parthenon, and Architecture, who holds a model of Hunt's Administration Building from the 1893 World's Colombian Exposition in Chicago.

The War Memorials

SEVENTH REGIMENT MEMORIAL

The funereal association of a memorial to fallen soldiers caused the board of commissioners to reject this monument when it was first proposed by the Seventh Regiment in 1867, as the aim of the Park was to "dispel . . . memories calculated to sadden or oppress."[22] Later that year it reversed the decision, and Ward was chosen by the regiment to create a new kind of war monument, one that honored the citizen–soldier, a volunteer, as opposed to the famous hero or professional officer of European war monuments.

A letter to Ward from Olmsted and Vaux in 1868 reveals that the designers of Central Park played a significant role in the creation of this monument.[23] They displayed as novel an approach to sculpture as they did to landscape

design, and one that is consistent with their commitment to the celebration of the common man. In the letter, the designers forcefully outlined their ideas for the figures, for the architecture of the pedestal, and for the placement of the monument in the Park. A small sketch in the letter depicted an eight-foot-high soldier at parade rest and dressed in the uniform of the regiment. Ward was instructed to have him "looking rather lonely and unsupported" atop an impressive base. They suggested that "two semi-recumbent figures . . . one of the tired soldier asleep and leaning on his arm, but with his musket at hand; the other of a soldier writing or reading a letter but fully equipped as if in expectation of an immediate call to action" support the main figure. These figures, while never executed for the final monument, were actually created in plaster by Ward to the specifications of the landscape architects.

One would naturally assume that it was Calvert Vaux, the creator of the thematic program for Bethesda Terrace, who suggested the statue's subject. That distinction more logically resides with Olmsted, however, who seven years earlier had accepted a position on the United States Sanitary Commission. The civilian organization was formed to monitor health and sanitary conditions of the Union troops and to act as advisers to the army's medical bureau. As Secretary General, Olmsted visited soldiers in the camps and hospitals and experienced firsthand the realities of military life. In his letters and reports, he expressed exasperation and disgust for the troops' lack of preparedness, the result of poor leadership and unprofessional conduct on the part of their officers. In a memorial to the common soldier, he understandably would have chosen to emphasize the prosaic aspects of military life while also stressing the ideal of a prepared and watchful soldier.[24]

When Olmsted and Andrew Haswell Green sited the monument on a small knoll overlooking the West Drive at

69th Street, just north of the Sheep Meadow, they were fully aware of the site's former importance in the original design submission.[25] In the Greensward plan, the meadow was intended to be a parade ground for military drills and practice—a stipulation in the competition. For their design Olmsted and Vaux created a dramatic Park entranceway for the troops in the form of a special military gate terminating on the present site of the monument. Nonetheless, after construction began, park commissioners and managers—Olmsted and Green among them—voted against any military use of the Park. By placing Ward's sentry above the meadow, Olmsted and Green were ensuring subtle but constant vigilance for the protection of their turf, though the regiment was afforded the novelty of marching in the Park for the monument's dedication ceremony.

Opposite: Ward's Seventh Regiment Memorial *(1869) had the most far-reaching influence of any post–Civil War sculpture. It became a prototype—along with a similar one by sculptor Martin Milmore—for future war memorials that are familiar in every town square across America.*

Above: The pose and attitude of the soldier for the Seventh Regiment Memorial *were suggested to the sculptor John Quincy Adams Ward in a letter, written by Olmsted and Vaux, which included the above sketch.*

Among the many sculptures in Central Park, Augustus Saint-Gaudens's masterpiece *William Tecumseh Sherman* of 1892–1903 is arguably the finest. The sculpture, which took the artist eleven years to complete (due, in part, to his operations for cancer), is as dazzlingly complex as the man he represents and as elusive to interpret as any great work of art. The work even mesmerized the artist himself, who considered it the crowning achievement of his life. Having received the Gold Medal at the Universal Exposition of 1899 in Paris, he wrote to his son Homer, "I have become a harmless, drooling, gibbering idiot, sitting all day long looking at the statue. Occasionally I fall on my knees and adore it."[26]

Dissatisfied with the traditional formula of horse and rider, the artist added the figure of Victory to the group, which set the tone for the entire piece. The artist worked and reworked the figure for years, changing models, drapery, and facial expressions until he achieved near perfection. Saint-Gaudens was criticized by some for juxtaposing the realism of Sherman and his horse with the idealized figure of Victory, while others criticized Victory for being too real a woman to be an ideal. Indeed, the figure's power seems to be its ambiguity; it represents both an actual woman—some say the artist's mistress, Davida Clark—and the perfection of classical female beauty.

Sherman is best known for his famous declaration, "War is Hell," a sentiment that is conveyed in the sculpture. The General looks both stoic and care-worn. He is reining in his horse; he wants it to stop, but the horse and Victory propel him onward. Underfoot, a Georgian pine bough has been trampled. The ambiguity of the real and the ideal is also present in the sculpture's dazzling golden skin.[27] Gold is not only the prize of war but also the price of war, the cost of countless deaths and destruction to the land. The glitter of victory on the surface belies the internal darkness of war within—in particular, Sherman's radically new psychological approach to war, which was merciless and total.

The General leans slightly forward into the wind. With shoulders squared, his hat in his hand, he sits rigidly in the saddle, a stern and stoic expression on his face. Man and horse are moving fast, Sherman's cloak and the horse's tail both flying in the wind. Sherman pulls tightly on the reins, causing the horse's wild expression—mouth open, eyes bulging, nostrils flared. Victory is the magnet that propels the group forward. The General's fluttering cape echoes the wings of Victory—he is the human embodiment of victory. Her forward motion parallels that of the horse and the man. Her toes just touch the very edge of the rock/pedestal. With one slight step, she could take flight. She resembles the most famous Victory allegory of all—the ancient Greek *Nike of Samothrace* in the Louvre, whose original position on the prow of a ship could have influenced Saint-Gaudens, for it was on display when the artist was studying in Paris.

In a daring tour de force, Victory's firmly closed Northern fist crushes a delicate Southern palm frond—the traditional symbol of peace—in the middle, much the way Sherman's army crushed Georgia and broke it in two. But her facial expression is as enigmatic as the smile of the Mona Lisa. Does her expression reflect the awe felt by the devastation of war? The only thing we know for certain is the artist's confirmation that his anti-war sentiments motivated him: "It is because I feel so strongly the damnation of the whole business of war, that I made it."[28] Saint-Gaudens, a young boy during the Civil War, grew up knowing both the passion and horror of war, and as an adult he watched Sherman become a living legend. In 1888, Saint-Gaudens was granted his wish to sculpt a portrait of his hero. The artist spent eighteen two-hour sittings with Sherman in order to produce his bust, which later became the head for the equestrian monument.

Southerners were naturally unappreciative of the statue of the man who destroyed their homeland. Their taunts aimed at the work included derogatory comments such as,

Sculptor Augustus Saint-Gaudens considered his last great sculpture, this memorial to Civil War General William Tecumseh Sherman, the finest achievement of his life. He fought to place it at the southern end of the Mall but finally agreed to its present location at the main entrance to the Park.

"Just like a Northerner to send a woman ahead of him—so nobody could shoot"; or, "who but a Northerner would let a woman walk while the man rides!" These detractors would have been shocked to learn that the first model for Victory was Hettie Anderson, an African-American woman from Georgia. She symbolized the emancipation from slavery— the one true victory of the war.[29]

Saint-Gaudens did not create his work for its present location. Architect Charles McKim, the collaborator on the base of the monument, specified that *Sherman* be placed at Grant's Tomb on Riverside Drive, an area of the city that McKim was promoting for development. The Grant family protested the siting of the statue near Grant's Tomb, and neither family—not the Grants nor the Shermans—wanted the other Civil War hero competing for attention. In 1886, the Grant family had initially requested the Mall in Central Park for the general's tomb. It took a great deal of persuasion to convince them to choose Riverside Park.[30]

Denied a spot near Grant's Tomb, Saint-Gaudens and McKim then requested the ever-desirable south end of the Mall. Landscape architect Samuel Parsons, Olmsted and Vaux's successor, considered the proposal "an artistic crime," because Saint-Gaudens and McKim planned a two- or three-acre space for balustrades and steps, which would have required felling many of the American elms.

If placed on the Mall, *Sherman* would have been near Ward's *Indian Hunter,* which Saint-Gaudens declared to be "a revelation"[31] and the most powerful influence on his early years as an artist. *Sherman* and the *Indian Hunter* share the forward-thrusting motion, the relationship of man and animal, and a psychological intensity.

Parsons, who had persuaded the Grants not to place the tomb either on the Mall or on the plaza at 59th Street, finally offered the prized spot to Saint-Gaudens. The artist accepted the site, but still insisted on the removal of some trees in order to better see his work. After long and delicate negotiations, park workers were sent to judiciously prune the offending branches. Gaetan Ardisson, the sculptor's life-long assistant, "plied them with whiskey and they became enthusiastic in their cutting—(alas, not enthusiastic enough)," Saint-Gaudens later complained.[32] In 1913, only six years after Saint-Gaudens's death, the plaza was greatly enlarged, allowing for a viewing distance much more in keeping with the artist's vision.

THE *MAINE* MEMORIAL

When the commissioners of the Park named the southwest entrance to the Park "Merchants' Gate" to honor the businessmen of the city, they could scarcely suspect that the gate would one day feature a monument to the greed and ambition of one merchant, newspaper publisher William Randolph Hearst—the man whose life was fictionalized in film by Orson Welles as "Citizen Kane." In his *Morning Journal*, Hearst developed what was known as "yellow journalism," characterized by sensational and frequently unethical news reporting and outrageous editorializing that more respectable newspapers avoided. Hearst and his rival, Joseph Pulitzer, publisher of the *New York World*, fought

The Maine *Memorial, donated by William Randolph Hearst, commemorates the sinking of the U.S.S.* Maine *in Havana Harbor during the Spanish-American War. Somewhat out of scale with the Park's romantic landscape, the monument was originally intended to be placed in Longacre—now Times—Square.*

head to head in fierce competition during the Spanish-American War, which was the conflict that inspired the *Maine* Memorial in Central Park.[33]

The reporting of atrocities—some true, some false—in Spanish-dominated Cuba ultimately led Congress to declare war on Spain in 1898. This boosted the *Morning Journal's* circulation to an all-time high and journalistic integrity to an all-time low. Within a year after Hearst took over the *Journal,* he dropped the price of the paper to a penny and increased the circulation six-fold. When artist Frederic Remington, hired as a special reporter, protested to Hearst that he could not draw nonexistent war scenes, his boss cabled the order, "You make the pictures, I'll make the war!" And Remington obeyed. After the sinking of the U.S.S. *Maine* in 1898, circulation rose to the million mark for the first time in American history, with Arthur Brisbane as editor-in-chief. (Brisbane has his own memorial and bench on the perimeter of the Park at Fifth Avenue and 101st Street.)

Four days after the U.S.S. *Maine* mysteriously exploded in Havana Harbor, killing 260 of the 350 men on board, Hearst suggested in the *Morning Journal* that the public begin a fund to honor the sailors. From schoolchildren's pennies to more substantial donations, the newspaper collected $100,000 in only a few months.[34]

Despite the immediate response of donations, siting the memorial was more difficult, and the delays were so protracted that Hearst was accused of absconding with the funds. At first Hearst suggested a monument far away from Central Park, "standing at the mouth of the Narrows, looking out over the ocean"—similar to the Statue of Liberty, already an American icon for twelve years. Eventually the current site of Times Square's TKTS tickets booth was selected, but due to a bureaucratic mix-up, a comfort station was erected there instead. When the Central Park site was established, architect Van Buren Magonigle—a former student of Calvert Vaux's—and sculptor Atillio Piccirilli real-ized the monument's inappropriate size for the Park site.[35]

The sculptures on the monument suggest overly complicated allegories that leave even the best art historians scratching their heads. Facing Columbus Circle, the youth on the prow of the ship, his hands held high in a victory sign, formerly held small bronze wreaths. On the front of the tall shaft is an allegorical group titled *The Antebellum State of Mind: Courage Awaiting the Flight of Peace and Fortitude Supporting the Feeble.* On the rear of the shaft is *The Post-Bellum Idea: Justice Receiving Back the Sword Entrusted to War.* The seated male allegory of Justice once held a bronze sword, which he was receiving from the female figure of War, but as the weapon is now absent, the meaning of the gesture is "missing the point."[36] In a tradition that dates back to ancient Roman fountains, recumbent male figures represent bodies of water, in this case Piccirilli's figures of the Atlantic and the Pacific. The gilded bronze figures of *Columbia Triumphant* and her seashell chariot led by three hippocampi (sea horses) are said to be cast from metals recovered from the guns of the ship itself.

Michele Bogart, in her brilliant analysis of late-nineteenth- and early-twentieth-century public sculpture, states, "as far as [the artists] were concerned, the sculptures simply glorified the values to which all citizens could or *should* relate," though they may never have done so.[37] The purpose of civic sculpture was to educate the growing urban immigrant population to an established set of preordained American values. But, as Bogart points out, these artists "worked very self-consciously within an elite . . . tradition whose representations and meanings had become . . . too exclusive to be fully effective." The hulking monument faces the taller, grandiose pillar of Columbus—both memorials represented beliefs at the turn of the century that social change would be affected by a display of monumental civic art works.

In his last will and testament, Joseph Pulitzer instituted the renowned Pulitzer Prize and also commandeered for himself the best prize in Central Park—the placement of his Pulitzer Fountain on the most coveted spot left in New York City. When Pulitzer was making out his will in May 1910, he already knew that Hearst had captured the site of Central Park's southwest corner for his *Maine* monument. Committed to fighting his rival even from the grave, the Austrian-born publisher made certain that he would control the most prominent site of all—the main entrance plaza for both Central Park and the Plaza Hotel.

Reaching its apogee at the turn of the century, Beaux-Arts urbanism and the related City Beautiful movement advocated a cityscape unified by broad avenues, sweeping vistas, and grand plazas featuring fountains, triumphal arches, and monumental sculptural projects as a way to solve urban problems and unite the burgeoning heterogeneous population. In this spirit, Karl Bitter, the Austrian-born architectural sculptor and protégé of Richard Morris Hunt, wrote an article in 1899 suggesting locations in the city that he felt needed such sculptural monuments. For Grand Army Plaza, unoccupied at the time, Bitter proposed a plaza and fountains like those at the Place de la Concorde in Paris. When Pulitzer died in 1911, leaving $50,000 for two symmetrical horseshoe-shape plazas modeled on those in the French plaza, he was no doubt influenced by Bitter's grand vision.

It is often quipped that Cornelius Vanderbilt II sold his mansion—which occupied the site of Bergdorf-Goodman at Fifth Avenue and 58th Street—when he took offense to his rear view of Karl Bitter's Pomona, the goddess of abundance, at the Pulitzer Fountain.

Not only did Pulitzer outsmart his archrival in garnering the Park's most coveted entrance, but he also had the last word on the man who hated newspapermen his whole life—William Tecumseh Sherman. The General, forever facing the Pulitzer Fountain across 59th Street, was known for his vituperative animosity toward members of the press: "Reporters are to me the most contemptible race of men that exist, cowardly, cringing, hanging around and gathering their material out of the most polluted sources."[38]

It was not surprising that Bitter chose to create the figure of Pomona, the Roman goddess of abundance. Popular for fountains of the Gilded Age, Pomona symbolized opulence and prosperity, and was an appropriate icon for the wealthy Plaza guests and residents of "Millionaires' Row" along Fifth Avenue.

For years people could only guess at the identity of the model for Pomona, but the secret was revealed in 1966 on the once-popular television show *I've Got a Secret.* Eighty-four-year-old Doris Discher Baum claimed that not only had she posed for the Pomona, but she was also the model for the Miss Liberty quarter first minted in 1916. It may be true, but perhaps in a flight of fancy she identified with Alice Butler from Windsor, Vermont, who was one of the models for Saint-Gaudens's Victory across the street as well as the classically profiled Liberty for his penny and ten- and twenty-dollar gold pieces.[39]

Central Park has no specific monument to the soldiers and victims who fought in World War II. That war is memorialized, however, by King Jagiello at Turtle Pond. In 1939, just as Hitler was about to invade Poland, New York City's World's Fair opened in what is now Flushing Meadows-Corona Park in Queens. For the entrance to the Polish Pavilion, the government chose Stanislaw Ostrowski's statue *King Jagiello.* Having defeated the German Teutonic Knights of the Cross in 1410 at the Battle of Grunwald, Jagiello symbolized the spirit of the Polish-Lithuanian nation in their victory over their hostile neighbor. Hitler intended to reclaim the land lost in Grunwald more than five hundred years earlier. Following victory over the Nazis, the exiled Polish government gave the statue to New York City in 1945 in memory of the bravery, courage, and loss of the Polish people. It is said that Jagiello crossed the two swords of his victims over his head as a sign of victory.

Stanislaw Ostrowski's King Jagiello (1939), memorializing the victory of the Polish-Lithuanian king over German forces in the 1410 Battle of Grunwald, was given to the Park in 1945 in recognition of the bravery of the Polish people against Hitler.

In 1950 a Cuban-American New Yorker began to promote the idea of a statue to Cuba's martyred hero, José Martí, who had died in 1895 fighting for Cuba's independence from Spain. Anna Hyatt Huntington, a sculptor of equestrians—including the *Joan of Arc* in Riverside Park—and a lover of Hispanic culture, agreed to create and donate the work for the cause. She completed the statue in 1959, but during ceremonies at the pedestal to honor Martí's birthday, in January 1960, both pro- and anti-Castro forces clashed over which group could claim the fallen hero as their own. The State Department made the decision to put the sculpture in storage until the political climate had changed. The statue was stored and the pedestal stood alone until 1965 when the work was unveiled in a peaceful and moving ceremony with the eighty-nine-year-old donor/artist present.[40] *José Martí* is the only sculpture in Central Park that is a monument to two wars: Cuba's liberation from Spain, and the ideological stalemate between the United States and Castro's Communist regime.

José Martí, *a monument to the martyred Cuban hero, was created and donated by sculptor Anna Hyatt Huntington.*

The sculptures in Central Park represent a wide range of cultures and diverse modes of artistic expression. On this page, Group of Bears by Paul Manship in the Pat Hoffman Friedman Playground.

The Animals

The Park has excellent examples of animals in the wild, a subject naturally appropriate for outdoor sculpture. The realistic depiction of animals began in France by a group of sculptors appropriately called *les animaliers*, who set the standard for the genre. The Park has two examples of these sculptures.

Created in 1850 by French artist Christophe Fratin and donated to the Park in 1863 by Gordon W. Burnham—the same man who donated *Daniel Webster* eleven years later—*Eagles and Prey* has the distinction of being the oldest sculpture in the Park. The sculptor worked in the newly revived lost-wax process of bronze casting, a technique particularly suited for the reproduction of realistic detail. Fratin showed a particular affinity for sculpting predators in the act of killing their prey. This was a startling new artistic viewpoint for a world on the brink of ascertaining Darwin's radical theories of evolution and natural selection. Here the artist presents two eagles savagely staking a claim on their next meal—a goat, caught between two rocks. The protruding tongue and bulging eyes of the unfortunate animal add a gruesome touch, so popular with an American public eager for realism in art. In *The Central Park,* published in 1864, author Fred Perkins writes enthusiastically, "The effect of waving wings and clinging vulturine attitudes is rendered with much success." Critics with a refined sensibility, such as Clarence Cook, thought such art out of tune with the uplifting and spiritual nature of the Park, so "apart from the purpose of noble art, whose aim is to lift the spirit of man to a higher region and feed him with grander thoughts."[41]

Today the sculpture seems randomly placed at the junction of two paths near the Mall, and its prominent pedestal tends to dominate the scene. In the nineteenth century, however, the pedestal was hidden by tall plants, which enhanced the realism of the gory drama. Furthermore, the site of the sculpture was originally an ideal spot, as the now-defunct Center Drive would have brought carriage riders eye-to-eye with the half-dead goat. New Yorkers would have seen in Fratin's sculpture a witty reference to these animals. At the time, the city was overrun with goats, dogs, and pigs—the only solution to the garbage problem before the Department of Sanitation was founded in 1866. "Gotham," New York's well-known epithet, actually means "goat-town" in old English. The commissioners' early reports complained, "The trees in the Park have already suffered much from these animals."[42] Guards were instructed either to place the scavengers in the Park's nearby pound or shoot them dead. So when the commissioners were required to site this sculpture, they might have placed it near the Mall as a talisman to protect the precious, new elm trees.

By the 1870s Park managers came up with a clever solution to harness the destructive goats that were overrunning the new landscape. Miniature goat-carts—advertised as "little rides for little people"— became a popular children's attraction on the Mall.

Opposite: A sculpture of two eagles anticipating a dying goat as their next meal caused some to criticize its suitability for a pastoral Park.

215

Left: In 1867, Tigress and Cubs by Auguste Cain was presented to Central Park by twelve gentlemen of New York. A tigress with tense muscles and sharp fangs proudly presents a dead peacock in her mouth to the young cubs, which eagerly await their next meal. The placement of the sculpture would have startled and amused Park viewers. The sculpture, now in the Central Park Zoo, was originally placed on a rock outcrop on Cherry Hill, which featured live peacocks in the early years of the Park.

Below: Still Hunt, a crouching panther perched on a ledge over unsuspecting joggers, is the Park's most surprising work of art.

Opposite: Without question, Balto, by American artist Frederick George Richard Roth, is the most popular animal sculpture in Central Park. The subject of the feature-length animated movie Balto (1995), Balto receives regular fan mail from school children enamored with this memorial to their beloved hero.

STILL HUNT

Americans soon began to emulate the *animaliers*, producing some of the most popular sculptures in Central Park. Sculptor Edward Kemeys, while serving as an axe-man during the early years of the Park's construction, took a passionate interest in the Zoo's animals. His fascination led him to become the foremost American animal sculptor of his time.

Kemeys' *Still Hunt* at 75th Street and the East Drive is a perfect example of how the site of a sculpture can also be an integral part of the work itself. A life-size, bronze panther crouches on a ledge of rock a few feet above the eye level of the Park visitor. The shock of surprise experienced by the unsuspecting viewer when encountering the realistic statue is the artist's intended reaction to its naturalistic placement.

BALTO

Created by American artist Frederick George Richard Roth, *Balto* is the most popular animal sculpture in Central Park. The statue commemorates a dog-sled relay that captured the attention of people throughout the world as they followed the dogs and their mushers on the radio and in the newspapers.[43] In January 1925, the city of Nome, Alaska, had a serious outbreak of diphtheria, and the supply of antitoxin was depleted. A relay was organized by the territorial governor, Scott Bond, to carry a twenty-pound package of serum almost seven hundred miles from the end of the railroad line at Nenana to Nome—normally a journey that takes at least twenty-five days by dog sled. The route followed the Iditarod Trail used by mail drivers from Anchorage to Nome (now the course of the dog-sled championships). The twenty teams of more than two hundred dogs covered the treacherous terrain at about six miles per hour, in blizzard conditions and at temperatures reaching fifty degrees below zero.

Champion sled-dog racer Leonhard Seppala and his fastest lead dog, Togo, were the first team to be tapped for the race. When it came time for his leg of the journey Seppala made a critical decision to take his dogs on a shortcut over frozen waters of the Arctic Sea, arriving only three hours before the ice floes broke.

It was Gunnar Kassen who chose Balto to lead his team for the final leg of the trip. Although Balto had been used by Seppala to haul freight, Kassen recognized the dog's leadership qualities. Just before daybreak on February 2, Balto led his team into the streets of Nome. The exhausting 674-mile journey was made in just over five days despite the forbidding conditions. The entire world was riveted to

In December 1925, only ten months after the famed sled relay, the monument to Balto by noted animal sculptor by Frederick George Richard Roth was dedicated in Central Park. The dog and his musher, Gunnar Kassen, in the squirrel-skin coat he had worn in the race, were present at the ceremony along with several dogs from the relay.

this remote corner of the world. Mistakenly, the *New York Times* reported on its front page, "Balto, Dog Hero of the Dash to Nome, Is Dead: Lungs of Leader and Other Dogs Were Frozen."

After the race, Hollywood producer Sol Lesser brought the famous dogs to California for the film *Balto's Race to Nome.* "Balto" dog food was soon a staple in dog-owning homes across America. But fame is fleeting; not long after the initial media blitz, Balto and his famous companions became lost in the world of sideshows and cheap "dime" museums. Two years later, the ill-treated dogs were purchased through a successful fund-raising campaign by the citizens of Cleveland, Ohio. On March 19, 1927 Balto, Fox, Skye, Old Moctoc, Billie, Tillie, and Alaska Slim, pulling the sled that carried the serum, paraded down the streets of Cleveland. They were given wonderful accommodations in the zoo until the end of their lives. Balto died on March 14, 1933. He is stuffed and mounted in the Cleveland Museum of Natural History.

Six years after the dedication ceremony, the Vaccination Research Association urged Mayor Jimmy Walker to remove the famous statue due to allegations by musher Leonhard Seppala that "the dash to Nome was a fake, pure and simple." Seppala, who actually lost a daughter in an earlier epidemic, claimed that he alone delivered the serum to Nome. Although his claims are an exaggeration of the truth, Seppala had successfully maneuvered his dogs over an extremely dangerous shortcut—a feat that was instrumental in the success of the relay. Understandably, he was bitter about receiving less recognition than he and his dogs deserved.

In 1932, a resolution to Seppala's grievance was found. Gimbel Brothers Department Store invited Young Togo, son of Seppala's lead dog, as a special feature for the Christmas season, and arranged a tribute to the entire relay team. Young Togo, harnessed to a Northern racing sledge, entered Central Park, mushed over the snow to the statue of Balto, and placed a wreath that read, "In memory of Balto, from Young Togo, whose father was also on the historic dash to Nome."[44]

The Playful Park

THE CRANE ALOFT SURVEYS THE WORLD ·· THE EARTHBOUND PEACOCK STRUTS AND BOASTS·

Above: In 1952 Paul Manship created one of the most whimsical and elegant sculptures in Central Park, the Osborn Gates for the William Church Osborn Memorial Playground that was just south of the Metropolitan Museum of Art. The gates depict several characters from Aesop's Fables such as the Crane and the Pelican (pictured), the Tortoise and the Hare, and the Country Mouse and the City Mouse. Weaving together Art Deco stylization, fanciful calligraphy, and an impeccable and elegant sense of design, Manship brilliantly captured the playfulness of childhood. The gates are now in storage and will be placed at the entrance to the Ancient Playground at Fifth Avenue and 84th Street when the playground is restored.

Paul Manship's Osborn Gates and Andrea Spadini's Delacorte Clock are two wonderful results of Commissioner Robert Moses's mission to enliven the Park with sculptures of fun and fantasy rather than those focused on important historical events, war, and ethnic heroes. Postwar America sought a return to innocence and leisure, and the public preferred a Park that was more a lighthearted place to play than an arena for political and military memorials. Moses brought that sense of childlike pleasure to the Park by the sculptures he placed there from 1934 until 1959, the penultimate year of his administration.

Left: The elephant from the whimsical Delacorte Clock, installed in 1964–65, recalls the clocks in medieval European public squares.

THREE DANCING MAIDENS

In its Conservatory Garden setting, this lively fountain, designed by Walter Schott in 1903, epitomizes the carefree spirit of youth. Yet the work itself was subjected to harsh circumstances before its placement in the Park.

In the early 1930s Hitler probably looked at *Three Dancing Maidens* (*Drei Tanzende Mädchen*) fountain every day. His chancellery was located across the street from the fountain, which stood in the courtyard of the mansion of Rudolf Mosse, the publisher of a liberal Berlin newspaper. Like countless other Jews, the Mosse family was forced to flee Germany, leaving everything behind. According to a letter by Rudolf's grandson, now an American citizen, their property was confiscated by the Nazis and probably sold to support the war effort.[45]

Three Dancing Maidens, *also known as the Untermyer Fountain.*

A bronze sculpture can have several casts.[46] This specific piece may be either a cast or the original sculpture itself, somehow smuggled out of Germany by Samuel Untermyer, an internationally prominent American lawyer and anti-Nazi activist. Photographs of the sculpture in front of the Mosse mansion show it to be on a base that is similar but not identical to the one in the garden; both are festooned with grotesque heads and garlands. It is unclear how the sculpture got to Greystone, the Yonkers, New York, estate of Untermyer, but it has been known as the "Untermyer Fountain" ever since it was donated to the Park after his death in 1947. Coincidentally, the fountain is placed on the site of the former cemetery belonging to the Congregation Shearith Israel of New York, the first Jewish congregation in the country.[47]

Bessie Potter Vonnoh originally created this fountain in 1926 as a central feature in a much larger conception, including an oval-shape, two-level garden, a nature-study center, and a storytelling area. It was to be called *The Secret Garden,* after the classic children's story, and dedicated to its author, Frances Hodgson Burnett. Only the central pool and the two figures were ever executed. Missing from the work is a Burnett inscription, intended in the original plan for the back of the storyteller's bench: "When you have a garden you have a future. When you have a future you are alive," a reason, perhaps, that it was eventually placed in the Conservatory Garden.

This charming fountain and birdbath, created in 1926 by Bessie Potter Vonnoh, is dedicated to Frances Hodgson Burnett, the author of The Secret Garden.

The original 1926 proposal for the Burnett Fountain called for a nature-study center and a storytelling area.[48] Eventually both functions were realized during the Moses administration, though not in conjunction with the Burnett memorial. The wooded promontory adjacent to the 59th Street Pond—one choice for the Burnett site—did become a nature sanctuary in 1934. The other site—the area west of Conservatory Water—became the Park's famous storytelling area when the Danish-American Women's Association donated a sculpture of Hans Christian Andersen by Georg Lober in 1956.

For a brief period in 1973, New Yorkers mourned the theft of the Ugly Duckling. The whole city was on the lookout for the sixty-five-pound duckling. One morning the Elmhurst, Queens, police precinct received an anonymous phone call reporting suspicious activity in an industrial area near Shea Stadium. Officers flooded the area with their searchlights until they found the sculpture in a brown paper bag atop a junk pile. Not exactly a fairy tale by Hans Christian Andersen, but certainly one with a happy ending.[49]

Lober's *Hans Christian Andersen* is unquestionably the direct copy of *Abraham Lincoln* done by Lober's teacher, Gutzon Borglum, the creator of the colossal Mount Rushmore presidents. Borglum created his seated Lincoln for the courthouse in Newark, New Jersey, where it stands today. Perhaps as an homage to his teacher, Lober seems to have copied Borglum's *Lincoln* soon after Borglum's death, although it seems that the sculpture's source has never been recognized.

Hans Christian Andersen *(1956)*
by Georg Lober (above) is very
similar to Abraham Lincoln *(oppo-*
site) by Lober's teacher, Gutzon
Borglum. Lincoln had always been
noted for his empathy, and the
artistic homage transfers Lincoln's
protective nature to Andersen's
similar parental one. Storytelling
on the monument's plaza has been
delighting children since the
sculpture was installed in 1956.

In 1932, eighty-year-old Alice Liddell Hargreaves, the namesake of the book *Alice in Wonderland,* came to New York as the guest of honor at the Lewis Carroll Centenary celebration at Columbia University. It is not known whether she visited Central Park, though given the English propensity for parks and gardens, it is quite likely that she did.[50]

Four years after Hargreaves's visit, Frederick George Richard Roth sculpted four of Carroll's famous characters on the central shaft of the Sophie Irene Loeb Fountain. One of the most beloved of all Central Park sculptures, *Alice in Wonderland* by Castilian-born sculptor José de Creeft, can be found only a short pathway from Roth's fountain.

De Creeft's personal work, in a style similar to that of his friend Picasso, focused on abstracted forms that represented the human figure; but in the *Alice* group the sculptor took a realistic approach. The Mad Hatter was a caricature of the work's donor, George Delacorte, and de Creeft's daughter was the model for Alice. However, the artist was told to alter the girl's face to match more closely the book's drawings by John Tenniel. Originally he had made his Alice a girl in her late teens, but he was instructed to make her "a child of twelve." The artist was also reminded in a letter from an aide to Commissioner Moses "to be sure she really looks like a little English girl."[51] The artist created a memorable face that evokes Tenniel's Alice while still having the universal appeal of girls everywhere.

Most people do not realize that there are two Alice in Wonderland *sculptures in Central Park: the famous one by José de Creeft and the Sophie Irene Loeb Fountain, originally adjacent to the Heckscher Playground and now in the James Michael Levin Playground. It was created by George Frederick Richard Roth, the sculptor of* Balto.

The most popular sculptures for children are those that are accessible. Alice in Wonderland *by José de Creeft and the near-by* Hans Christian Andersen *by Georg Lober almost always have children climbing on them.*

Environmental and Conceptual Art

In the mid- to late twentieth century some artists looked to the land for raw materials, inspiration, and spirituality that they felt were missing from contemporary art. It was in the context of the environmental art movement that Central Park became appreciated as the prototype for earthworks, not only by landscape architects and historians, who had always known that the Park was a masterpiece, but also by the broader art world. Robert Smithson considered Central Park America's first earthwork. Mourning the decrepit condition of Olmsted's masterpiece in 1973, he envisioned a conceptual piece that would not only re-create the original art processes of the designer but also help to restore Central Park *and* another needy park or landscape in the fiscally impoverished city. "Maintenance on the Pond seems long overdue," he wrote. "The mud should be dredged out. This maintenance operation could be treated in terms of art, as a 'mud extraction sculpture.' . . . The mud could be deposited on a site in the city that needs 'fill.'"[52] Unfortunately Smithson died only a few years later, and his "mud piece" remained only an informal conception until the recent restoration by the Central Park Conservancy. Smithson's contemporaries, Claes Oldenburg and Christo and Jeanne-Claude, created more formalized art works for the Park.

While anti-Vietnam protests were raging daily on the Sheep Meadow in the 1960s, artist Oldenburg created a conceptual sculpture titled, *Placid Civic Monument,* which was, among other things, an anti-war statement.

Oldenburg's concept nullified brilliantly the traditional war memorial while offering a new and powerful work of art. On October 1, 1967, gravediggers were hired to create a six-by-three-foot hole near the Obelisk, a monument describing the military victories of the Pharaoh. The negative space simultaneously implied both the negation of a monument and the suggestion of a grave of a fallen soldier. Furthermore, Oldenburg's monument was created in the shadow of the Metropolitan Museum of Art, the sanctum sanctorum of the art establishment. Once the work was photographed and documented, the artist filled in the hole—remembrance and forgetting as one.[53]

In 1967 artist Claes Oldenburg created Placid Civic Monument, *which was, among other things, a protest to the Vietnam War.*

Christo and Jeanne-Claude. *The Gates, Project for Central Park, New York City.* Collage, 2002. Pencil, fabric, wax crayon, charcoal, pastel, and aerial photograph

The Gates, first proposed in 1980 by Christo and Jeanne-Claude, were envisioned as free-hanging, saffron-colored fabric banners that would hang above most of the paths in Central Park. The artists intended the work to be temporarily exhibited in the Park for two weeks during the winter months.

227

With the creation of Strawberry Fields,[54] Central Park incorporated a landscape that is both a conceptual artwork and a new form of memorial. John Lennon's widow, Yoko Ono, wrote, "In memory of John Lennon, New York City has designated a beautiful triangle island in Central Park to be known as Strawberry Fields. . . . John would have been proud that this was given to him . . . rather than a statue or a monument."[55]

The land—planned in the 1860s to be the area for the Refectory, the Park's major restaurant—was officially adopted as a memorial to Lennon by the City Council on March 26, 1981. The designation was introduced by Manhattan Councilman-at-Large Henry J. Stern and ratified by a majority of the city, despite an attempt to thwart the effort by Republican minority leader Angelo Arculeo, who felt that Lennon did not deserve the distinction since crooner Bing Crosby, an "American folk hero," had not been honored when he died.[56]

Ono, a conceptual artist, initially thought to plant English and Japanese plants, representing their respective homelands, but then she remembered a more symbolic act that she and John had performed when they first met. "We planted an acorn in England as a symbol of our love. We then sent acorns to all the heads of state around the world, inviting them to do the same. Many responded saying that they enjoyed the experience." That concept led to Ono's August 28, 1981 ad in the *New York Times* requesting gifts from around the world, in Lennon's memory. Countries were invited to "offer plants, rocks and/or stones of their nations. . . . The plants will eventually be forests, the rocks will be a resting place for travelling souls, the bricks will pave the lane John and I used to walk on and the circle where we used to sit and talk for hours."

Immediately gifts started pouring in from around the world: a tile bench from the Moroccans, a fountain from the French, a huge amethyst from the Paraguayans, and a totem pole from the Aleutian Indians. These traditional monuments were returned by the Parks Department to their respective donors. Instead, a new landscape—one sensitive to the Greensward vision of Olmsted and Vaux—was created by Yoko One in tandem with Bruce Kelly, a landscape architect with expertise in Olmsted landscapes. Countries were represented by living plants rather than by monuments, an approach that was sensitive to the initial mission of the Park. A plaque on a rock outcrop along the east–west path of Strawberry Fields lists the 121 countries that wished to be remembered by plants in Lennon's memory. Conceived as an international garden where visitors can imagine a peaceful world, it is a place where Jordan's fothagilla, for example, grows beside Israel's cedar.

The woodland slope of Strawberry Fields in autumn. "It will be nice to have the whole world in one place, one field, living and growing together in harmony." Those words used by Yoko Ono to describe Strawberry Fields also echo and reinforce the vision for the creation of Central Park.

229

Above: People leave a few coins and make a wish, as if the Imagine medallion were the Trevi Fountain. Two of the most moving and poignant days in Central Park are the anniversary of John Lennon's birth, October 9, and his death, December 8. At the dedication on October 9, 1985 Yoko Ono, quoting "Hey Jude," said, "It is our way of taking a sad song and making it better." Lennon touched the lives of people everywhere, and they come every day with flowers, letters, photographs, and more unusual gifts—a pair of red high heels, a baseball, a school notebook, a box of strawberries from the neighborhood deli. The only permanent artifact of Strawberry Fields is the Greco-Roman–style mosaic, the gift of the Italian government. Ono worked with landscape architect Bruce Kelly to design the circular mosaic. "Since we have a Lenin Square in the world, I would like to have a Lennon Circle," she said. The land itself is in the shape of a teardrop and has become an impromptu memorial to those who had untimely deaths: fellow Beatle George Harrison, Linda McCartney, Jerry Garcia, Jim Morrison, Marilyn Monroe, Elvis Presley, Janis Joplin, Jimi Hendrix, Mama Cass Elliot, and Princess Diana.

Opposite: In fall 2002, the public was invited to participate in a bulb planting dedicated to the memory of the World Trade Center victims.

If you would seek his monument, look around you.
  —Sir Christopher Wren's tombstone epitaph

Despite Olmsted and Vaux's vehement opposition to memorials in the Park, nonetheless, in 1860 they proposed to erect a bust in the Ramble to ANDREW JACKSON DOWNING, who they wanted to honor for his contribution to the formation of the Park.[57] An urn designed by Vaux eventually came to be placed on the Mall—the one in Washington, D.C.—that Downing was in the process of designing when he drowned. Vaux also memorialized his mentor by the greatest tribute of all, naming his first son Downing Vaux.

Olmsted and Vaux also worked together on the design for Downing Park in Newburgh, New York, though it was only completed in 1897 by their children Downing Vaux and John Charles Olmsted—who, along with Frederick Law Olmsted, Jr., followed their fathers' footsteps into the profession of landscape architecture. In 1899 Downing and the Olmsted brothers were also three of the founders of the American Society of Landscape Architects.

After Central Park, Calvert Vaux and Frederick Law Olmsted collaborated on many more public parks: Prospect

Park in Brooklyn, Riverside and Morningside Parks in Manhattan, and parks and park systems in Albany, Buffalo, Newark, Providence, Fall River, and Chicago, along with the residential suburban community of Riverside, Illinois, and the Niagara Reservation. The professional partnership of the two designers ended in 1872.

CALVERT VAUX maintained an intermittent professional connection with Central Park for the remainder of his life, though he would frequently call upon his former partner to come to the aid of the Park during serious threats to their original design. Nonetheless, Vaux was angry and frustrated throughout his life by the increasing credit that Olmsted continued to receive for their Central Park work.

His tragic death—considered a suicide by the Vaux family—occurred near a Brooklyn pier on a foggy November morning in 1895. The seventy-one-year-old designer, depressed and lonely after the death of his beloved wife, Mary, possibly took his own life by throwing himself into the same river that had taken the life of his mentor. He was lovingly remembered by the Park commissioners, who sent plants from Central Park to his private funeral. [58] The only existing memorial to Vaux is the apartment building "The Vaux" just outside the Park on West 97th Street and next door to "The Olmsted." You can read their names on the doormats.

FREDERICK LAW OLMSTED'S son reported his father's regret that a "mistake" had been made by the city fathers in choosing the central site over the Jones Wood site along the East River.[59] Nonetheless, probably no other landscape or project meant as much to the famous designer as Central Park. Writing to Vaux from California in 1865, he revealed the importance that the Park held: "There is no other place in the world that is home to me. I love it all through and all the more for the trials it has cost me."[60]

The beautiful planting bed between Shakespeare and Columbus was dedicated to Frederick Law Olmsted in 1972, on the 150th anniversary of his birth. Olmsted was a prolific writer and publisher and, therefore, merits a place on Literary Walk, ironically the very spot that he fought to protect from all other memorials.

At the end of his life, Olmsted suffered from depression and erratic behavior that would today be diagnosed as dementia. The world-famous landscape architect lived out his last years as a patient in a celebrated psychiatric institution, the McLean Hospital in Waverly, Massachusetts, the grounds of which he had previously designed. Expressing his disappointment and frustration, he railed against the hospital for siting the buildings in a different manner than proposed in his original conception: "They didn't follow my plan, confound them."[61]

Though Olmsted died the same year as his old nemesis ANDREW HASWELL GREEN, the 1903 Department of Parks' *Annual Report* gave Green a fitting tribute while completely ignoring the passing of the man who had changed the face of New York City's parks and parkways. Green had become the Controller of New York and was responsible for profoundly shaping the city's future. Called "the Father of Greater New York," he fought for the consolidation of the five boroughs, which was finally realized in 1898. His death was, perhaps, the most tragic of all. At age eighty-three, he was murdered on the steps of his home by a deranged gunman, Cornelius Williams, who mistook the civic leader for another white-haired and bearded man with a similar name. Green is remembered by a bench, dedicated in 1929 and located in the upper Park at 104th Street on the site of a former War of 1812 redoubt, Fort Fish. It is an appropriate location, as Green was an early preservationist who fought to save and recognize important sites in American history.

EGBERT VIELE, passed over for the design of Central Park (and a few years later for the design of Prospect Park) by Olmsted and Vaux, lived an active life late into his years and even became a Park commissioner from 1883 to 1884. In 1864, Viele had sued the city, claiming that the two creators of the Greensward plan had stolen his design. He knew that some features of the Greensward plan, particularly the transverse roads, had appeared in his design that had been adopted by the first Central Park commission. While Olmsted and Vaux had split the $2,000 prize, Viele walked away from his court case almost $9,000 richer, mainly as compensation for having created the first plan. In his testimony, Viele proudly told the court that he had entered the competition with two designs, one signed (entry #28) and one that he had purposely forged to prove that the commissioners were biased and predisposed to choose other candidates.[62] There is no written submission that compares with Viele's acknowledged entry, though the confession of duplicity may reveal the secret to the most mysterious submission to the competition.

When the commissioners opened the envelope for entry #2, they found a drawing of a pyramid with no further explanation or signature.[63] As the pyramid was only the second entry received, it must have been a knee-jerk response to the announcement of a competition, an unofficial rejection of Viele's adopted plan. Pyramids were common tomb forms in the nineteenth century. Their association with reincarnation and eternal life equated ancient Egyptian beliefs with Christian ones—and Egbert Ludovicus Viele's thirty-one-foot-high granite pyramidal tomb in the Old Cadet Cemetery at West Point stands solidly today as evidence of the general's lifelong obsession with the afterlife and the symbolic pyramids.[64] Viele's most long-lasting and useful contribution was his topographic map of Manhattan Island, so accurate that it is still in great demand today. A visionary in his own right, he was one of the earliest designers of an underground subway system for New York City.

The Egyptian-style railings that surround the Obelisk were JACOB WREY MOULD's last work in Central Park. In the 1870s the bohemian artist left New York rather abruptly due perhaps to some sort of illegal or underhanded financial dealings—not surprising after his years with the Tweed administration. Mould spent some years in Lima, Peru, where he designed buildings and parks, and then returned to the New York Parks Department, where he was responsible for Grant's first tomb on Riverside Drive. Shunned publicly for living with an unmarried woman, the brilliant designer is buried alone in Brooklyn's Greenwood Cemetery.

The other sculptor of Bethesda Terrace, EMMA STEBBINS, is buried only a short walk from Mould. She, too, lies without the eternal companionship of her beloved Charlotte Cushman, though her tombstone does acknowledge her importance as "a beloved sister and a faithful friend." Ironically, the artist of the *Angel of the Waters* fountain is memorialized by a drinking fountain for dogs in Lenox, Massachusetts, where she lived alone during her last years, with the little dog that she and Cushman had both deeply loved.

It is somewhat fitting that RICHARD MORRIS HUNT has the most lavish monument of the Park builders. In the end his vision of civic grandeur triumphed on 59th Street, the site of the proposed Beaux-Arts gates that Olmsted and Vaux detested. Olmsted and Hunt went on to collaborate on many important projects, including the Vanderbilts' Biltmore estate in North Carolina and the World's Columbian Exhibition in Chicago. Vaux and Hunt, who died within four months of each other, remained on cordial personal terms throughout their lives. In 1869, New York erected its first apartment building, designed by Hunt and fashioned on the model of "French flats" promoted by Vaux twelve years earlier. Hunt's building, the Stuyvesant at 145 East 18th Street, was immediately popular with the city's intellectual and artistic crowd, and Calvert Vaux was one of the first tenants to sign a lease.[65]

Surprisingly, after the demise of the Tweed Ring, ROBERT J. DILLON continued to serve on the board with Olmsted, Green, Stebbins, and Frederick Church until his death a year later. In his obituary, the *New York Times* acknowledged his contribution to the design of Central Park, stating that "to his suggestion is due the construction of many of the most delightful parts of the Park."[66] Amen.

The lasting tribute to Central Park itself was its recognition as a National Historic Landmark by the federal government in 1965 and as New York's first scenic landmark by New York City in 1974. This status ensures future generations that Central Park, one of America's greatest works of art and the world's first democratically driven urban park, created "of the people, by the people, and for the people shall not perish from the earth."

Much loved, the landscape of Central Park is often looked upon as a singular achievement, 843 acres miraculously reserved from the relentless march uptown of the Manhattan grid plan adopted in 1811 by municipal officials as the immutable blueprint for developing New York City's real estate. But it is much more than that. Observed both at home and from abroad as the cynosure of the burgeoning commercial and industrial metropolis, Central Park quickly became a model for other cities' metropolitan parks and an important catalyst in the nineteenth-century parks movement. A manifestation of the Western impulse toward social democratization beginning in the eighteenth century, the public park

enfranchised urban populations with commonly accessible pleasure grounds for health and recreation. Royal parks originally established as hunting preserves by the Crown had been gradually opened to such use in European cities; Central Park was a purpose-built people's park with an intended moral purpose growing out of, and reinforcing, American republican values. Its success as a city-planning experiment in social and political terms quickly made it worthy of emulation.

Although, as the foregoing text makes clear, Frederick Law Olmsted and Calvert Vaux's original Greensward plan was somewhat amended in the give-and-take of the political arena and its planned uses

modified by changing cultural circumstances, Central Park still functions in many respects as its designers intended. And it continues to offer valuable lessons in the art of landscape design. Olmsted and Vaux themselves applied those lessons to the creation of Brooklyn's Prospect Park.

Like Central Park, Prospect Park weds engineering technology and nature into such artful synthesis that many people assume its features are natural rather than naturalistic. Like its predecessor, Prospect Park employs grade

separation of various types of circulation to ensure safe, fluid movement of different modes of traffic. Because of the designers' participation in the selection of the park site, it has a generously configured lake and an unparalleled passage of extensive, rolling meadow scenery, successfully creating an illusion of open countryside in the middle of otherwise dense urban fabric.

The Brooklyn park marks the genesis of the designers' metropolitan planning vision. Pleasurable movement by carriage, horseback, and on foot along functionally dedicated routes through interesting scenery could, they reasoned, be extended outside the park's boundaries. They convinced the Brooklyn board of commissioners to build Eastern Parkway and Ocean Parkway, Prospect Park's boulevard-like extensions, which served as tree-planted spines for future residential development.

Calvert Vaux considered Central Park "a magnificent opening" for the growth of urban parks in America. In 1865 he used those words in a letter to Frederick Law Olmsted—far away in California at the time—urging his partner to return to New York to collaborate on the new Brooklyn park. The Long Meadow in Prospect Park is arguably the greatest example of their vision of a limitless greensward.

Because the design intention of Central and Prospect Parks was to represent rural scenery, people often overlook the degree to which Olmsted and Vaux were committed to innovative technology. They early grasped the possibilities that technology offered for making the entire city more agreeably parklike. They understood how transportation by suburban rail and trolley lines and the invention of macadam paving, facilitating swift travel by carriage, encouraged the separation of commercial districts and residential neighborhoods. In Buffalo, New York, Olmsted and Vaux created a park-and-parkway system, and in Riverside, Illinois, they designed an entire suburb with curvilinear tree-lined streets, which they connected to Chicago by means of a parkway. Olmsted, who later practiced with his sons after dissolving his partnership with Vaux, designed a park-and-parkway system within the rolling hills and valleys of Louisville, Kentucky. He was instrumental in conceptualizing and building Boston's Emerald Necklace, a park system extending from the Boston Common to Franklin Park.

It is ironic that the technological infrastructure and management means for creating and sustaining Olmstedian park scenery—grade-separated circulation, underground water-supply and drainage systems, topographical grading, topsoil replenishment, judicious tree removal as well as tree planting, and myriad tasks involving lawn care and ongoing structural repairs—should be so generally invisible that many people assume that the great nineteenth-century parks are simply nature reservations and that they will thrive with only minimal human intervention. Absent recognition as landmark landscapes, such artfully designed and carefully engineered parks have often been treated as commodities, lands temporarily reserved from the process of design and development, mere open spaces ready to receive an array of worthwhile monuments and structures of a recreational and cultural nature, available as well to yield to demands by commercial and institutional interests.

It is understandable that the agendas of these later generations—agendas of sports recreation, mass entertainment, and political activism—should have been accommo-

dated within these great public spaces. But it is too bad that the promoters and planners of so many heterogeneous encroachments should ignore so completely the original park designers' intelligently conceived view lines, circulation systems, planting plans, and water-body configurations, or that they should have been allowed to exploit these in limited ways that compromise the integrity of the parks' overall designs. Beginning in the mid-1970s, the confluence of the burgeoning environmental protection movement and the historic preservation movement engendered a new perspective on the status of public parks. Civic leaders became aware of the fact that park landscapes are both built and natural and that they require professional care by trained managers who understand how to mediate the interests of users while conserving the landscapes and preventing their overuse and abuse. What had been tolerated in the laissez-faire 1960s, when both rules and management standards were abandoned, could not continue if parks were to survive. Following the lead of New York's Central Park Conservancy, in one city after another citizens began to form public–private partnerships, forging alliances with mayors and parks departments, creating boards of directors, developing management and restoration plans, engaging in fund-raising for park renovation.

Along with the renewal of historic parks has come the building of new parks, particularly along riverfronts and harbors, the sites of many abandoned industrial and port facilities. One hopes that these will become the much-loved heritage parks of a future generation. They will if they are created with the same grand vision and attention to detail that Olmsted and Vaux brought to their work as city planners and park designers, and if they are loved enough by constituents who realize that cyberspace is not a substitute for public space and that great parks are an important continuing public responsibility of cities and their citizens.

Elizabeth Barlow Rogers is the founder, first president, and life trustee of the Central Park Conservancy and the director of Garden History and Landscape Studies at the Bard Graduate Center for Studies in the Decorative Arts, Design, and Culture.

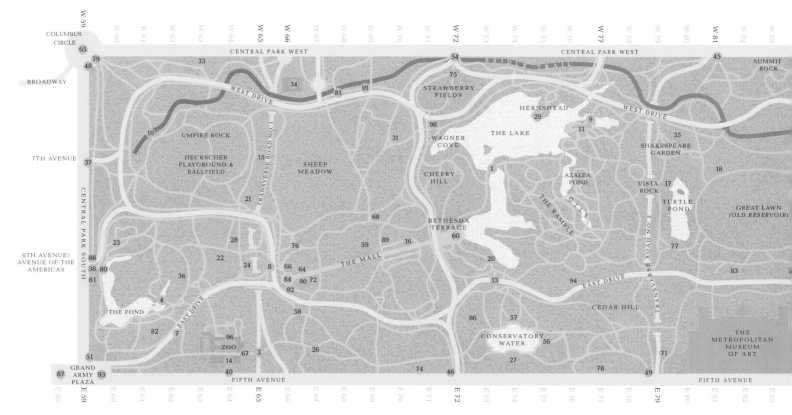

The features mentioned or depicted in the book are shown on the map.

ARCHES AND BRIDGES

1. Bow Bridge (W. 73)
2. Bridge no. 28 (W. 94)
3. Denesmouth Arch (E. 65)
4. Gapstow Bridge (E. 62)
5. Glen Span Arch (W. 102)
6. Huddlestone Arch (E. 105)
7. Inscope Arch (E. 62)
8. Marble Arch (*demolished*, E. 65)
9. Oak Bridge (*now* Bank Rock, W. 77)
10. Pinebank Arch (W. 62)
11. Ramble Arch (W. 77)
12. Springbanks Arch (W. 102)
13. Trefoil Arch (E. 73)

ARCHITECTURE

14. Arsenal (E. 64)
15. Ballplayers' House (*demolished,
    now* Ballplayers' Concession, W.65)
16. Bandstand (*demolished*, E. 69)
17. Belvedere Castle (W. 79)
18. Berceau Walk (*demolished*, W. 82)
19. Blockhouse (W. 109)
20. Boathouse (*demolished*, E. 73,
    now Loeb Boathouse, E. 74)
21. Carousel (W. 65)
22. Children's Cottage (*demolished*) (E.64)
23. Cop Cot (E. 60)
24. Dairy (E. 65)
25. Dana Discovery Center (E. 110)

26. Dene Shelter (E. 67)
27. Kerbs Boathouse (*proposed Conservatory site*)
28. Kinderberg (*demolished, now* Chess
    and Checkers House, E. 64)
29. Ladies Pavilion (W. 75)
30. Maze (*demolished*, E. 84)
31. Mineral Springs Pavilion
    (*demolished*, W. 70)
32. Mount St. Vincent Museum and
    Restaurant/McGown's Pass Tavern
    (*demolished*, E. 105)
33. Paleozoic Museum (*proposed site*) (W. 63)
34. Sheepfold (*now* Tavern on the Green, W. 66)
35. Swedish Cottage (W. 79)
36. Wollman Rink (E. 63)

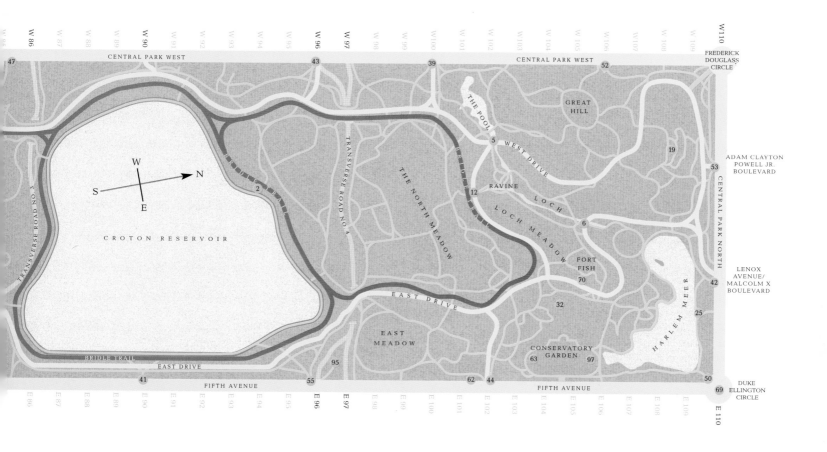

NAMED GATES

37. Artisans' Gate (W. 59 & 7 Ave)
38. Artists' Gate (W. 59 & 6 Ave)
39. Boys' Gate (W. 100)
40. Children's Gate (E. 64)
41. Engineers' Gate (E. 90)
42. Farmers' Gate (W. 110 & Lenox Ave)
43. Gate of All Saints (W. 96)
44. Girls' Gate (E. 102)
45. Hunters' Gate (W. 81)
46. Inventors' Gate (E. 72)
47. Mariners' Gate (W. 85)
48. Merchants' Gate (W. 59 & CPW)
49. Miners' Gate (E. 79)
50. Pioneers' Gate (E. 110)
51. Scholars' Gate (E. 60)
52. Strangers' Gate (W. 106)
53. Warriors' Gate (W. 110 & Adam
 Clayton Powell, Jr. Blvd.)
54. Women's Gate (W. 72)
55. Woodman's Gate (E. 96)

SCULPTURES AND MONUMENTS

56. Alice in Wonderland (E. 75)
57. Hans Christian Andersen (E. 74)
58. Balto (E. 67)
59. Ludwig van Beethoven (E. 70)
60. Bethesda Fountain (E. 72)
61. Simon Bolívar (E. 59)
62. Arthur Brisbane bench (E. 101)
63. Burnett Fountain (E. 104)
64. Robert Burns (E. 66)
65. Christoforo Columbo (Russo)(W. 59)
66. Christopher Columbus (Suñol)(E. 66)
67. Delacorte Clock (E. 65)
68. Eagles and Prey (E. 69)
69. Duke Ellington (E. 110)
70. Andrew Haswell Green bench (E. 105)

71. Group of Bears (E. 79)
72. Fitz-Greene Halleck (E. 67)
73. Alexander Hamilton (E. 83)
74. Richard Morris Hunt Memorial (E. 70)
75. Imagine (W. 72)
76. Indian Hunter (E. 66)
77. King Jagiello (E. 80)
78. Sophie Irene Loeb Fountain (E. 77)
79. Maine Memorial (W. 59)
80. José Martí (E. 59)
81. Giuseppe Mazzini (W. 67)
82. Thomas Moore (E. 61)
83. Obelisk/Cleopatra's Needle (E. 81)
84. Olmsted Bed (E. 66)
85. The Osborn Gates (future E. 85)

86. Pilgrim (E. 72)
87. Pulitzer Fountain (E. 59)
88. José de San Martín (E. 59)
89. Johann C. F. von Schiller (E. 70)
90. Sir Walter Scott (E. 66)
91. 7th Regiment Memorial (W. 69)
92. William Shakespeare (E. 66)
93. William Tecumseh Sherman (E. 59)
94. Still Hunt (E. 77)
95. Albert Bertel Thorvaldsen (E. 97)
96. Tigress and Cubs (E. 64)
97. Untermyer Fountain (E. 105)
98. Daniel Webster (W. 72)

Endnotes

ABBREVIATIONS:

BCCP, *Annual Report:* Board of Commissioners of
the Central Park, *Annual Report of the Board of
Commissioners of the Central Park,* 1857–70. (To
avoid confusion, the date cited reflects the year
for which the text reports rather than the year
the report was published—most often in January
of the following year.)

BCCP, *Minutes:* Board of Commissioners of the
Central Park, *Minutes of Proceedings of the
Board of Commissioners of the Central Park*
(New York, 1857–70).

Cook, *A Description:* Clarence Cook, *A Description
of the New York Central Park* (New York, 1869;
rpt. 1979).

Country, Park & City: Francis R. Kowsky, *Country,
Park & City: The Architecture and Life of Calvert
Vaux* (New York, 1998).

*Description of Plans: Description of Plans for the
Improvement of Central Park* (New York, 1858).

DPP, *Annual Report:* Board of Commissioners of the
Department of Public Parks, *Annual Report of
the Board of Commissioners of the Department
of Public Parks* (New York, 1871–74).

DPP, *Minutes:* Board of Commissioners of the
Department of Public Parks, *Minutes* (New York,
1871–98; some years are unavailable).

The Empire of the Eye: Angela Miller, *The Empire of
the Eye: Landscape Representation and
American Cultural Politics, 1825–75* (Ithaca,
1993).

FLOP: Frederick Law Olmsted Papers, Manuscript
Division, Library of Congress.

Forty Years: Frederick Law Olmsted Jr. and
Theodora Kimball, eds., *Forty Years of
Landscape Architecture: Central Park*
(Cambridge, MA, 1973).

Nature and Culture: Barbara Novak, *Nature and
Culture: American Landscape and Painting,
1825–75* (New York, 1980).

The Park and the People: Roy Rosenzweig and
Elizabeth Blackmar, *The Park and the People*
(Ithaca and London, 1992).

PFLO: The Papers of Frederick Law Olmsted, ed.
Charles MacLaughlin, vols. 1–6, Supplementary
Series, vol. 1 (Baltimore, 1977–97).

FLO: Frederick Law Olmsted

CV: Calvert Vaux

INTRODUCTION

1. Simon Schama, *Landscape and Memory* (New
York, 1995), 61.

2. Robert Smithson, "Frederick Law Olmsted and
the Dialectical Landscape," *Artforum* XI, no. 6
(Feb. 1973): 65, 68.

3. FLO to BCCP, Letter of Resignation, Jan. 22,
1861, *Forty Years,* 310. See also BCCP, *Sixth
Annual Report* (1862), 37.

4. BCCP, *Fifth Annual Report* (1861), 48.

5. FLO & CV, *A Review of Recent Changes, and
Changes which have been Projected in the Plans
of the Central Park,* Letter I, "A Consideration of
Motives, Requirements and Restrictions
Applicable to the General Scheme of the Park"
(Jan. 1872), *Forty Years,* 248.

6. Quoted in *Nature and Culture,* 226.

7. Edward Johnson, *Wonder-Working Providence*
(1654), J. Franklin Jamison, ed. (New York, 1910);
quoted in William Cronon, *Changes in the Land*
(New York, 1983), 5.

8. *Empire of the Eye,* 210.

9. Ibid., 13.

10. CV to Clarence Cook, June 6, 1865, FLOP, also
quoted in *The Park and the People,* 150.

11. See "Statement of the Quantity of certain
Classes of Work done and of Materials used in
the Construction of the Central Park, exclusive
of Operations on the General Water Works of
the City," DPP *Third Annual Report* (1874),
350–1.

12. FLO & CV, *A Review of Recent Changes,* Letter
II, "Examination of the Design of the Park and of
Recent Changes Therein," (Feb. 1872), *Forty
Years,* 268.

CHAPTER 1

1. In 1999, Park Commissioner Henry J. Stern completed the work begun in the 1950s by his predecessor Robert Moses to chisel the names of the
eighteen original gates into the wall of the Park.

2. The Standing Committee on Statuary, Fountains
and Architectural Structures delivered its *Report
on Nomenclature of the Gates of the Park* on
Apr. 10, 1862 to the full board of commissioners.
BCCP, *Sixth Annual Report* (1862), 125–36.

3. "Yeoman," *New-York Daily Times,* Jan. 12, 1854,
"The South," quoted in Charles Capen
McLaughlin et al., *PFLO,* vol. II, "Slavery and
the South 1852–1857," 240.

4. Ibid., 240.

5. "Report on Nomenclature," 128.

6. Edward K. Spann, *The New Metropolis: New
York City 1840–1857* (New York, 1981), 135.

7. Ibid., 35–44.

8. Andrew Jackson Downing, "The New York
Park," *Horticulturist* 6 (Aug. 1851); quoted in
BCCP, *First Annual Report,* doc. no. 5 (Jan. 19,
1857), 164.

9. Originally the state legislature enacted a bill
that included the land from 59th Street to 106th
Street as well as the Jones Wood site, a 150-acre
site along the East River, for a total of more than
900 acres. By 1854 the Jones Wood section was
revoked. The Central Park site, originally 778
acres, was expanded in 1863 for the final total of
843 acres (see the map on page 78). The 1853
document does not officially name the Park, but
does dictate the creation of "the Central Park
Fund"; see "An Act to Alter the Map of the City
of New York, By Laying Out Thereon a Public
Place, and to Authorize the Taking of the Park,"
in BCCP, *First Annual Report,* doc. no. 5, 89.

10. "Nomenclature Report," 128.

11. Quoted in Edwin Burrows and Mike Wallace,
Gotham: A History of New York City to 1898
(New York, 1999), 792.

12. FLO to BCCP, *Documents of the Board of
Commissioners of the Central Park for the Year
Ending April 30, 1859,* doc. no. 5 (May 31, 1858),
6.

13. *Description of Plans,* FLO and CV, "Greensward:
Description of a Plan for the Improvement of
Central Park," 35.

14. Letter from FLO to Charles Loring Brace, Dec. 1,
1853, *PFLO,* vol. II, 235.

15. FLO, "Public Parks and the Enlargement of
Towns," *Forty Years,* 171.

16. Robert H. Byer, "Words, Monuments, Beholders:
The Visual Arts in Hawthorne's *The Marble
Faun,*" in David C. Miller, ed., *American
Iconology* (New Haven, 1993), 167.

17. *Humboldt* was placed in the Park in 1869 on the
west side of Scholar's Gate near the entrance
steps to the Pond. It was moved in 1982 and is
now sited across from the American Museum of
Natural History at Central Park West and
Seventy-seventh Street.

18. *PFLO,* vol. III, 180–81.

19. *American Carriages,* 69.

20. Clarence Cook, *A Description,* 84.

21. Rob[er]t J. Dillon and August Belmont, *The New
York Herald,* June 7, 1858, 1.

22. CV to Clarence Cook, June 6, 1865, FLOP; CV to
FLO, June 3, 1865, FLOP.

23. FLO, "Public Parks and the Enlargement of Towns," quoted in Melvin Kalfus, *Frederick Law Olmsted: The Passion of a Public Artist* (New York, 1990), 291.

24. Dell Upton, "Inventing the Metropolis," *Art and the Empire City: New York, 1825–1861* (New York, 2000), 43.

25. Another straight line is formed by the East Drive from 85th Street to 94th Street; however, that line is the result of a lack of space rather than being a pure design decision. There was also a straight walk, known popularly as "Lover's Lane," that disguised, as best as possible, the southern and western walls of the rectilinear reservoir; see also *Forty Years*, 221, note 1.

26. *New York Times*, Nov. 11, 1858, 1.

27. I am grateful to Marianne Cramer for bringing this interpretation of the Mall—and so much more—to my attention.

28. *Nature and Culture*, 3.

29. FLO to Mary Olmsted, *PFLO*, vol. III, 19.

30. FLO to Pilat, *Forty Years*, 347.

CHAPTER 2

1. Calvert Vaux, *Villas and Cottages: A Series of Designs Prepared for Execution in the United States* (New York, 1857; 2nd ed., 1864, rpt. New York, 1970), 43. See *Country, Park and City*, Chapter 5, for the most complete description to date of the carvings, their execution, and their possible sources. "The Heart of the Park" was first used in *The Central Park: Photographed by W. H. Guild, Jr. with Descriptions and A Historical Sketch by Fred. B. Perkins* (New York, 1864), 16.

2. David T. Van Zanten, "Jacob Wrey Mould: Echoes of Owen Jones and the High Victorian Styles in New York, 1853–1865," *Journal of the Society of Architectural Historians* 28 (1969): 41–57.

3. The first mention of Mould is as draughtsman, paid $70.50 on December 3, 1858, BCCP, *Second Annual Report* (1858), 46 (first illustration of the Terrace), 58.

4. See BCCP, *Sixth Annual Report* (1862), 62–65.

5. The plan is signed "C. Vaux," leaving no uncertainty that he is the author. Cook notes that "busts of distinguished Americans" were also intended for the Terrace, *A Description*, 48. When this was proposed is not specified, but it was never mentioned in any of the commissioners' annual reports.

6. Stephen Jay Gould, "Church, Humboldt, and Darwin: The Tension and Harmony of Art and Science," Franklin Kelly, et al., *Frederick Edwin Church* (Washington, DC, 1989), 97.

7. For Humboldt's influence on Vaux's mentor, Andrew Jackson Downing, see Judith K. Major, *To Live in the New World: A. J. Downing and American Landscape Gardening* (Cambridge, MA, 1997), 139–40.

8. Alexander von Humboldt, *Cosmos: A Sketch of A Physical Description of the Universe,* translated by E. C. Otté, vol. 2 (New York, 1850; rpt. Baltimore, 1997), 98.

9. See, Ellwood C. Parry III, *The Art of Thomas Cole: ambition and imagination,* (Newark, DE, 1988), 226, for possible literary sources for Cole's cycle.

10. Howard S. Merritt, *Thomas Cole* (Rochester, 1969), 35.

11. According to the commissioners' annual reports for the years 1860 through 1868, the first carvings, completed about 1860, were those that featured abstract ornamentation on the facades of the arcade under the 72nd Street Drive, also known as Bridge #1. By January 1862 the carvings on the staircase balustrades, their terminal piers, and the screen of piers grouped across the Terrace esplanade were completed. The four large seasonal panels at the top of the stairways were completed by 1867, and all of the Terrace carvings were finished by 1868.

12. See, Michael Wilson, *William Kent: Architect, Designer, Painter, Gardener 1685–1748* (London, 1984), 214.

13. Suggestions to the author that the pentagram might be connected to the Masonic order have been considered. I am grateful to Thomas Savini, director of the Chancellor Robert R. Livingston Library and Museum, Masonic Hall in New York for confirming that the configuration of stars on the Terrace is not an emblem of the Masonic order.

14. BCCP, *Eighth Annual Report* (1864), 25.

15. For illustrations that show the changes to the plan see: BCCP, *Second Annual Report* (1858), 58; BCCP, *Third Annual Report* (1859), 38. In June, 1860 Olmsted reported that the archway of the Terrace "should be very simple . . . [and] could possibly be built for $7000 or $7500," a probable indication that the commissioners were interested in a less elaborate design, BCCP, *Minutes* (June 8, 1860), 7. By January 1863 when the *Sixth Annual Report* was published, the board of commissioners recognized the Terrace

as "the central and main architectural structure of the Park, to which all others were intended to be subordinate, and being, with its connections, the principal place for pedestrians, it seemed fitting that an expenditure should here be made commensurate in some degree with the important relative position that this structure was to hold," BCCP, *Sixth Annual Report* (1862), 33. A request for the freestanding seasonal sculptures is mentioned in BCCP, *Minutes* (Dec. 11, 1862), 49. The models are described by Mary Garland, Stebbins's sister, as "Studies ordered by the Park Commissioners of the Seasons to be placed on the pedestals arranged for such figures, on the steps descending from the 'Mall' on the Central Park," in the Emma Stebbins Scrapbook, Archives of American Art, Smithsonian Institution, Washington, DC.

16. Burrows and Wallace, *Gotham*, 876.

17. A photograph by W. H. Guild in *The Central Park* shows an American flag flying atop Vista Rock from the wooden tower that predated Belvedere Castle.

18. CV to Cook, June 6, 1865, FLOP.

19. Ibid.

20. Richard Morris Hunt, *Designs for the Gateways of the Southern Entrances to the Central Park*, Chapter III: [W. Hoppin], "A Letter to the Commissioners of the Central Park," 1866, 16. Hunt's conception was most likely influenced by the plan of H. Noury, the eighth entrant to the design competition, whose monumental gateways were very similar (see *Description of Plans*, no. 8).

21. See *PFLO*, vol. III, note 13, 271.

22. BCCP, *Seventh Annual Report* (1863), 10.

23. Montgomery Schuyler quoted in Van Zanten, "Jacob Wrey Mould," 41, note 7. Olmsted took a temporary leave of absence from his work on the Park during the Civil War to become the Secretary of the U.S. Sanitary Commission, though he returned periodically to work with Vaux. In 1863, he left Washington to manage the Mariposa Mines in California and did not return to New York until November 1865.

24. BCCP, *Eighth Annual Report* (1864), 26–27.

25. [Daniel Wise], *Little Peachblossom: or Rambles in Central Park* (New York, 1873), 40.

26. "God is light, and in Him is no darkness at all. The love of light is more instinctive in the human heart than any other desire connected with beauty." John Ruskin, *Modern Painters*, vol. 2 (1873), 26.

27. "In placing the grain and the cottage near the spade and the scythe, the artist may have meant

to say that from industry come plenty and comfort," [Wise], *Little Peachblossom*, 40–41.

28. Burrows and Wallace, *Gotham*, 873.

29. Paintings such as Winslow Homer's *Veteran in a New Field* and George Inness's *Peace and Plenty*, both painted in 1865 and both in the Metropolitan Museum of Art, reinforce the wheat field as a symbol of the North's victory over the South as well as the abundance of America and the return to the work of peace time.

30. "[T]he Bible, lamp, and hour glass, obeyed in time secures us a happy life forever. A beautiful thought whether the sculptor meant it or not." [Wise], *Little Peachblossom,* 40.

31. Quoted in Roger B. Stein, *John Ruskin and Aesthetic Thought in America, 1840–1900* (Cambridge, MA, 1967), 73.

32. John Ruskin, *The Seven Lamps of Architecture* (1880; rpt. of 2nd edition, New York, 1989), 4.

33. Burrows and Wallace, *Gotham,* 749.

34. I am grateful to Rita Powell for suggesting this interpretation.

35. Mould had a particular interest in folklore; as a poet and lyricist, he had set his poem, "The Sea King's Bride," about the Scandinavian water-king Necken, to music by Jakob Ahlstrom.

36. See BCCP, *Eighth Annual Report* (1864), 7.

37. Much of Stebbins's work is lost, but a scrapbook of her work in the Archives of American Art of the Smithsonian Institution, Washington, DC, contains photographs of a variety of sculpted angels that she had created, such as *Sandalphon,* a "child's angel."

38. The printed announcement is in the Stebbins Scrapbook; see also DPP, *Third Annual Report* (1873), 8.

39. According to J. E. Wrigley, *Catholic Encyclopedia,* vol. B, "Bethesda," 347, (Washington, DC, 2003), "Excavations have revealed the outlines of a large, oblong pool provided with five porches, 4 lateral and a fifth central to divide the pool into two parts." Wrigley's entry also cites J. T. Milik [*Revue Biblique* 66 (1959) 347–48] who believes that "Bethesda" is from *byt´ šdtyn* in the reading of the Copper Scroll (11.12) found among the Dead Sea Scrolls, which he translates as "a rectangular double reservoir." On nineteenth-century excavations, see W. D. Davies, Eric M. Meyers, and Sarah Walker Schroth, *Jerusalem and the Holy Land Rediscovered: The Prints of David Roberts (1796–1864)* (Durham, NC, 1996), 116. In the submissions by H. Hoffman and C. Wehle to the

design competition, the authors proposed "a high monument representing a figurative image of the Croton river pouring water on the city," for a location between the two reservoirs; see *Description of Plans,* "The New York Central Park, According to the Design of H. Hoffman and C. Wehle," entry no. 31, 9.

40. Susan E. Cayleff, *Wash and be Cured: The Water-Cure Movement and Women's Health* (Philadelphia, 1987), 2.

41. A bottle of Bethesda Springs water is on exhibit at the New Orleans Pharmacy Museum. The label depicts an angel hovering over a round basin of water with the cupola of a building in the background.

42. Marilyn Symmes, *Fountains: Splash and Spectacle: Water and Design from the Renaissance to the Present* (New York, 1998), 88.

43. FLO to John Olmsted, Nov. 15, 1860; quoted in Laura Roper, *FLO: A Biography of Frederick Law Olmsted* (Baltimore, 1973), 151.

44. Henry James, *William Wetmore Story and His Friends* (Boston, 1903; rpt. New York, 1957), 257.

45. Lillian Faderman, *Surpassing the Love of Man: Romantic Friendship and Love between Women, from the Renaissance to the Present* (New York, 1981), 16.

46. Elizabeth Milroy, "The Public Career of Emma Stebbins: Work in Marble," *Archives of American Art Journal* 33, no. 3 (1993): 4 and note 14, 11–12.

47. A photograph of the pedestal for Stebbins's bust of Cushman in the Stebbins Scrapbook reveals that the artist placed a bas-relief of an angel embracing personifications of "Comedy" and "Tragedy"—the traditional symbols for actors—directly beneath the bust of the actress.

48. Henry T. Tuckerman, *Book of the Artists: American Artist Life* (New York, 1867), 603.

49. Milroy, "The Public Career of Emma Stebbins: Work in Bronze," *Archives of American Art Journal* 34, no. 1 (1994): 11.

50. A poem by Oliver Wendell Holmes written in 1861, just after the attack on Fort Sumter, uses the metaphor of healing water for a "darkened" country; see *Empire of the Eye,* 10.

51. Vaux, *Villas and Cottages,* 43.

52. Ruskin, *The Seven Lamps of Architecture,* 217.

53. DPP, *First Annual Report* (1871), 15–16. No photographs of the flooring and ceiling together are known to exist, though there is a reference to them in DPP, *Minutes* (May 29, 1878), 54. In 1986, during routine maintenance by the Central Park Conservancy, a few broken pieces of floor tile were uncovered at the northern threshold of the

arcade, though their design was not similar to the one on the ceiling. The Central Park Conservancy will begin the complete restoration of the entire ceiling in 2004.

54. Historian John Howat states that the statue was on exhibit in the Park's Mount St. Vincent Museum; see John K. Howat, "Private Collectors and Public Spirit: A Selective View," *Art and the Empire City: New York 1825–1861* (New York, 2000), 102–03, from information in Tuckerman, *Book of the Artists,* 313; The commissioners comment, however, that "The Statue of Flora, by Crawford, presented by the late R. K. Haight, Esq., has not been delivered at the Park," in BCCP, *Ninth Annual Report* (1865), 42, and there is no mention of the sculpture in any subsequent annual report. It is presumed that the sculpture was never presented to the Park after Haight's death.

CHAPTER 3

1. For the relationship through marriage of Olmsted to Bryant, see *PFLO*, vol. III, 59–63.

2. See *The Park and the People,* 15–36.

3. Andrew Jackson Downing, "A Talk about Public Parks and Gardens," *Horticulturist* (Oct. 1848); "The New York Park," *Horticulturist* (Aug. 1851).

4. CV to FLO, June 3, 1865, FLOP.

5. *Walks and Talks of an American Farmer in England* (1852), *A Journey in the Seaboard Slave States* (1856), and *A Journey through Texas* (1857); see *PFLO*, vol. II, "Slavery and the South: 1852–1857" (Baltimore, 1981).

6. Quoted in *PFLO*, vol. 3.

7. Rebecca Bedell, *The Anatomy of Nature: Geology & American Landscape Painting, 1825–1875* (Princeton, 2000), 91–94. See also Malcolm Andrews, *Landscape and Western Art* (New York, 1999), 131.

8. Like the future Central Park, a Brown landscape was, according to Simon Schama, an "affectation of naturalism . . . for in order to achieve the effect of 'pure' landscape, whole hills had to be leveled or raised, lakes dug, and mountains of manure carted to the estate," *Landscape and Memory,* 540.

9. Egbert Viele, "The Plan," *First Annual Report for the Improvement of the Central Park* (New York, 1857), 36.

10. Ibid., 37–38.

11. Ibid., 39.

12. According to Samuel Parsons, the successor to Olmsted and Vaux as landscape architect,

"[S]everal plans and models that constituted part of this competition ... were to be seen in the Arsenal in Central Park, less than twenty years ago," Mabel, Parsons, ed., *Memories of Samuel Parsons: Landscape Architect of the Department of Public Parks, New York* (New York, 1926), xviii. See also, Gregory F. Gilmartin, *Shaping the City: New York and the Municipal Arts Society* (New York, 1995), 253–54, for discovery and restoration of the original Greensward plan and documents in the Arsenal. The Waring drawing is cited in the collection of the New-York Historical Society in *The Park and the People*, note 38, 553. A four-part paper negative of the original is in the collection of the Frances Loeb Library, Graduate School of Design, Harvard University. See also [William Alex], *The Central Park: Original Drawings* (Frederick Law Olmsted Assoc., 1980).

13. The required written description for entry no. 4 suggests a more conventional and credible design. Rink informed the commissioners that he had entered three different plans in the Preface of his written entry. The depicted plan (no. II) was described as a "green color finished plan." *Description of Plans*, entry no. 4, 1.

14. Central Park Conservancy's arborist Neil Calvanese and landscape architect Chris Nolan confirmed the truth of Gustin's claim.

15. See *PFLO*, vol. III, 345–52.

16. The choice of using "Olmsted and Vaux" rather than the reverse merely reflects the spoken and written conventions of the past. It is not meant to reflect the importance of Olmsted over that of Vaux. See *The Park and the People*, 434–35, 598, note 65.

17. FLO and CV, "Proposition to Place a Colossal Statue at the South End of the Mall," quoted in *Forty Years,* 494.

18. Quoted in *Sixth Annual Report of the Board of Commissioners of Prospect Park, Brooklyn* (1866), 23.

19. From a document titled "Calvert Vaux Duly Sworn" (1864), FLOP; quoted in *City, Park & Country*, 122.

20. Charles E. Beveridge and Paul Rocheleau, *Frederick Law Olmsted: Designing the American Landscape* (New York, 1995), 34.

21. Quoted in Leo Marx, *The Machine in the Garden* (New York, 1964), 236.

22. Olmsted evoked a portion of the psalm in his written description for Prospect Park. Olmsted, Vaux & Co., "Report of the Landscape Architects" (Jan. 1, 1868), in Brooklyn Parks Commission, *Annual Reports* (1861–73), 91; FLO,

"Public Parks and the Enlargement of Towns," in *Civilizing American Cities: A Selection of Frederick Law Olmsted's Writings on City Landscape,* ed. S. B. Sutton (Boston, 1979), 81. E. & H. T. Anthony & Co. to Lincoln, Jan. 7, 186[3], The Abraham Lincoln Papers, Library of Congress.

23. FLO to Ignaz A. Pilat, Sept. 26, 1863, *Forty Years,* 343–49.

24. "Architecture, American Institute of Architects," *The Crayon* 6 (June, 1857): 218; "Parisian Buildings for City Residents," *Harper's Weekly* 1 (Dec. 19, 1857): 809–10.

25. See Vaux's quote in Elizabeth Hawes, *New York, New York: How the Apartment House Transformed the Life of the City, 1869–1930* (New York, 1993), 24.

26. A typescript describing Andrew Haswell Green's role in the creation of Central Park and his career as comptroller—evidently part of a larger work probably written by Henry Mann and "received and corrected" by Green and submitted to him on March 7, 1903, eight months before his death—cites the former commissioner's opinion that the transverse roads were "especially [Vaux's] idea and creation." Andrew Haswell Green Papers, New-York Historical Society. In the Prefatory Notes by John Foord, *The Public Life and Service of Andrew Haswell Green* (New York, 1913), Mann's contributions are verified and acknowledged.

CHAPTER 4

1. The commissioners' request that Olmsted recommend modifications to his design "arising from other plans exhibited or from his own reflections," BCCP, *Minutes* (May 13, 1858), 23–24. See BCCP, *Documents of the Board of Commissioners of the Central Park for the Year Ending April 30, 1859* (New York, 1859), doc. no. 3, and BCCP, *Minutes* (May 27, 1858), 52, for Olmsted's replies.

2. See BCCP, *Minutes* (May 18, 1858), 38–39, and (May 24, 1858), 44–47, for Dillon's proposed amendments. *The New-York Daily Times*, May 13, 1858, 10, although strongly supporting the Greensward plan, also complimented many other plans, coincidentally no. 26 by Howard Daniels, who had proposed the single straight avenue favored by Dillon and Belmont. The printed text that accompanied the exhibition of the thirty-three plans is bound into one volume,

Description of Plans for the Improvement of Central Park, (New York, 1858), in the New-York Historical Society; see also *The Park and the People*, note 38, 553–54.

3. See *Description of Plans*, no. 22; Rob[er]t J. Dillon and August Belmont, *New York Herald,* June 7, 1858, 1.

4. Dillon and Belmont, *Herald*, 1.

5. *Description of Plans*, [Samuel Gustin], "Explanatory Notices of a Design for Laying Out the Central Park," entry no. 30, 7.

6. See *Description of Plans*, "Greensward," 35.

7. BCCP, *Seventh Annual Report* (1863), 38.

8. BCCP, *Twelfth Annual Report* (1868), 35; see also Cook, *A Description,* 1994–95.

9. By 1911, the Traffic Squad of the New York City Police Department was permitted to hold an exhibition and review drill on the Sheep Meadow, while thousands looked on. In 1917 a captured German submarine, the UC-5, was transported to the Sheep Meadow along with a British tank in order to arouse interest in the World War I Liberty loans. Harry Truman's 1945 Navy Day speech on the Meadow was the first televised presidential press conference.

10. *New York Tribune,* May 5, 1933.

11. FLO & CV, "A Consideration of Motives, Requirements and Restrictions Applicable to the General Scheme of the Park." Letter I, Jan., 1872, *Forty Years,* 250.

12. FLO, "Superintendent of Central Park to Gardeners,' c. 1873, *Forty Years,* 358.

13. Edward Hagaman Hall, *McGown's Pass and Vicinity* (New York, 1905), 9.

14. *Description of Plans*, "Greensward," 232.

15. See *Description of Plans*, "Explanatory Notes of a Design for Laying Out the Central Park, no. 30," 11; or, those by entries nos. 15, 22 (Charles Graham and J. A. Bagley), or 27 (Howard Daniels). BCCP, *Minutes* (May 24, 1858), 46.

16. A rendering by either Vaux or Mould of the structure first appeared in the BCCP, *Fifth Annual Report* (1861), 47, and was republished in the DPP, *First Annual Report* (1871), 25, as a different drawing by Mould.

17. FLO & CV to H.G. Stebbins, Letter I, *Forty Years,* 251–52.

CHAPTER 5

1. Beveridge and Rocheleau, *Frederick Law Olmsted*, 35.

2. FLO, "Music from the Water," *Forty Years,* 414.

3. BCCP, *Minutes* (Feb. 6, 1862), 91, 93. My grati-
tude to Sharon Flescher for locating a photograph of the Café Musard in Michel Cabaud,
Paris et les Parisiens sous le Second Empire
(Belfond, 1982), 238.

4. During the American Revolutionary War from
1776–83, British and Hessian troops constructed
fortifications on the sites, which were rebuilt in
1814. See the unpublished report for the Central
Park Conservancy by Richard Hunter et al.,
Hunter Research, Inc., *A Preliminary Historical
and Archeological Assessment of Central Park to
the North of the 97th Street Transverse, Borough
of Manhattan, City of New York*, vols. I and II
(1990).

5. Martina D'Alton, *The New York Obelisk or How
Cleopatra's Needle Came to New York and What
Happened When it Got Here* (New York, 1993),
11, 45.

6. I am grateful to Frank Kowsky for the information on Vaux views, correspondence with author,
August 15, 2002.

7. *New York Times*, June 16, 1958, 22.

8. Simon Schama, *Landscape and Memory*, 376.

9. Martina D'Alton, *The New York Obelisk*, 22, 63.

10. BCCP, *Tenth Annual Report* (1866), 38–39.

11. Humphrey Repton, *Fragments on the Theory and
Practice of Landscape Gardening* (London, 1816).

12. Fields made a motion to discount entry no. 33 on
the basis of its failure to meet the March 31st
midnight deadline. He was overruled. BCCP,
Minutes (April 28, 1858), 188.

13. Dillon resigned from the old Board in 1858, when
he lost support for his insistence that all work on
the Park be contracted out to the lowest bidder.

14. All following quotes and information on the
Tweed administration are taken from *First
Annual Report of the Board of Commissioners of
the Department of Public Parks for the Year
Ending May 1, 1871* (New York, 1871). See also
New York Times, Nov. 25, 1872, 1–3.

15. William F. Mangels, *The Outdoor Amusement
Industry* (New York, 1940), 61.

16. Charlotte Dinger, "The Stein and Goldstein in
Central Park," *Carrousel Art* 1 (Garden Grove,
CA, 1980), 27. I am grateful to manager Sal
Napolitano, who has been involved with the
Carousel since 1970 and provided information
from past managers.

17. BCCP, *Fifth Annual Report* (1861), 23.

18. *New York Times*, Mar. 7, 1871, 5. I am grateful to
Carol Spawn of the Academy of Natural
Sciences, Philadelphia, for her attention to my
interest in Hawkins.

19. For a complete discussion of the social and mili-
tary history of the pre-Park site, see Edward
Hagaman Hall, *McGown's Pass and Vicinity*
(New York, 1905).

20. *The Metropolitan Museum of Art Annual
Reports of the Trustees of the Association,
1871–1902*, Eighth Annual Report (New York,
1878), 128.

21. FLO & CV to Stebbins, Letter II, *Forty Years*, 267.

22. FLO & CV to Stebbins, Letter I, *Forty Years*, 251.

23. *Forty Years*, 205.

CHAPTER 6

1. FLO to Richard Grant White; see David Schuyler
et al., *PFLO*, vol. VI, 101.

2. *Forty Years*, "Report of Committee of Statues in
the Park," Apr. 25, 1873, 488–93. See also Cook,
A Description, 77–78.

3. Wayne Craven, *Sculpture in America* (Newark,
DE, 1984), 250; see also 226.

4. See clippings from *Commercial Advertiser*, Nov.
8, 1865; Sordello, *The Evening Post*, "The New
Statue: J. Quincy Ward's 'Indian Hunter,'" Nov.
3, 1865, in the John Quincy Adams Ward
Scrapbook, Albany Institute of History and Art
Library.

5. See Lewis Sharp, *John Quincy Adams Ward:
Dean of American Sculpture* (Newark, DE,
1985), fig. 3, 19.

6. Quoted from an unidentified and undated clipping in the Ward Scrapbook.

7. Sharp, *John Quincy Adams Ward*, 27. I am grateful to Michele Bogart for suggesting Ward's
ambivalence toward Native Americans, in personal correspondence with the author, July, 2002.

8. *New York Times*, May 24, 1872, 2; also quoted in
an undated clipping, "Ward's Statue of
Shakespeare," *The Christian Union*, in the Ward
Scrapbook; see also *Shakespeare: Ward's Statue
in the Central Park* (New York, 1873).

9. Charles Colbert, *A Measure of Perfection:
Phrenology and the Fine Arts in America*
(Chapel Hill, 1997), 224.

10. Lawerence Levine, "Order, Hierarchy and
Culture," *Highbrow/Lowbrow*, 222. See also
Colbert, *A Measure of Perfection*, 218–22.

11. Levine, *Highbrow/Lowbrow*, 221–22.

12. See reviews in the contemporary press for attitudes regarding the inferior physiognomy of
native Americans and the "confirmation" of
these disparaging attitudes in Ward's sculpture,
Ward Scrapbook.

13. Robert H. Byer, "Words, Monuments, Beholders:
The Visual Arts in Hawthorne's *The Marble
Faun*," quoted in David C. Miller, *American
Iconology*, 325, notes 6 and 7.

14. Ibid., 166.

15. Rule no. 3 stipulated that statues "commemora-
tive of men or of events of far reaching and permanent interest shall be placed on the Mall,"
quoted in *Forty Years*, 493.

16. In 1876, after the placement of Webster, the committee added the stipulation that "Statues to be
placed on the Mall shall be of bronze, and of
heroic size. Colossal statues shall not hereafter
be placed in the Park," quoted in *Forty Years*,
493; see also, FLO and CV, "Proposition to Place
a Colossal Statue at the South End of the Mall,"
Forty Years, 494–98.

17. See Colbert, *A Measure of Perfection*, 201–03.

18. See *New York Times*, Nov. 23, 1880, 1. For an
account of the fire see Gerald T. Koeppel,
Water for Gotham: A History (Princeton, 2000),
174–77.

19. *Thorvaldsen* was originally placed at Artizans'
[sic] Gate at 59th Street and Seventh Avenue.

20. Gilmartin, *Shaping the City*, 9.

21. *New York Times*, Aug. 15, 1973, 41. See also
Gilmartin, *Shaping the City*, 248–49.

22. BCCP, *Eleventh Annual Report* (1867), 31.

23. FLO & CV to Ward, Ward Archives, cm 544, box
1, folder 8, Albany Institute of Art and History
Library.

24. See *PFLO*, "Defending the Union," vol. IV (1986);
see also Laura Wood Roper, *FLO: A Biography
of Frederick Law Olmsted* (Baltimore, 1973),
chap. 15–20.

25. *Description of Plans*, "Greensward," 18–19. In
keeping with the nomenclature program of the
gates, FLO and CV suggested the statue be put
at Warrior's Gate at 110th Street and Seventh
Avenue; see Ward Archives, Albany Institute of
History and Art. See also Emmons Clark, *History
of the Seventh Regiment* (New York, 1890), vol.
II, 155.

26. Augustus Saint-Gaudens, *The Reminiscences of
Augustus Saint-Gaudens*, edited and amplified
by Homer Saint-Gaudens (New York, 1913), vol.
2, 136.

27. "Gold against Bronze: Should the Sherman
Monument Have Been Gilded or Let Alone?"
New York Times, June 21, 1903, 8. See also Henry
James's comments quoted in Burke Wilkenson,
The Life and Works of Augustus Saint-Gaudens
(New York, 1985), 327; and the Nov. 15, 1908 letter
to Homer Saint-Gaudens from William Dean

Howells about the real and the ideal in Saint-Gaudens's work, quoted in *Reminiscences,* 62.

28. Saint-Gaudens's response of Feb. 8, 1906 to Henry James, quoted in Saint-Gaudens, *Reminiscences,* 299.

29. Louis Hall Tharp, *Saint-Gaudens and the Gilded Era.* (Boston, 1969), 322; Saint-Gaudens, *Reminiscences,* quoted in John Dryfhout, *The Work of Augustus Saint-Gaudens,* 219. See also www.sgnhs.org, the website of the Augustus Saint-Gaudens National Historic Site, Cornish, New Hampshire.

30. Saint-Gaudens, *Reminiscences,* vol. 2, 294–96. See Mabel Parsons, ed., *Memories of Samuel Parsons,* 96–97, for a discussion of the Grant family; for the account of *Sherman,* see Chapter XIII, "Location of Sherman Statue," 100–04.

31. Saint-Gaudens, *Reminiscences,* vol. 2, 52; see also Sharp, *John Quincy Adams Ward,* 47.

32. Saint-Gaudens, *Reminiscences,* vol. 2, 296.

33. See Michele H. Bogart, *Public Sculpture and the Civic Ideal in New York City 1890–1930* (Washington, 1997), 185–217.

34. Gilmartin, *Shaping the City,* 244–45.

35. For objections by the Art Commissions and their final acceptance of the monument see Bogart, *Public Sculpture,* 201–02.

36. I thank Charles Kipps for this witty comment.

37. Bogart, *Public Sculpture,* 230.

38. Michael Fellman, *Citizen Sherman: A Life of William Tecumseh Sherman* (Lawrence, KS, 1985), 126.

39. Eve Brown, *The Plaza 1907–1967* (New York, 1967), 53; Tharp, *Saint-Gaudens and the Gilded Era,* 316, 319, 357.

40. *New York Times,* Oct. 10, 1964, 31; Oct. 16, 1964, 38; Jan. 27, 1965, 34.

41. Cook, *A Description,* 73.

42. *Forty Years,* 33, note 4.

43. The most complete narrative of the rescue can be found in Ellen M. Dolan, *Susan Butcher and the Iditarod Trail* (New York, 1993). See also *New York Times,* Jan. 28 to Feb. 11, 1925.

44. *New York Times,* Sept. 25, 1931, 32; Sept. 29, 1931; Dec. 22, 1932, 15. I am grateful to Jonathan Kuhn for sharing with me a Parks Department press release of a dog-sled race held in Central Park on Feb. 22, 1934 that included Togo.

45. Correspondence to Central Park Conservancy, May 25, 1994.

46. A recent letter to the New York City Department of Parks & Recreation, dated July 5, 2001, noted a similar sculpture in the Schlosspark at Burg Schlitz, in Mecklenburg-Vorpommern, Germany.

The author of the letter cites a guidebook to the Castle, indicating that Schott created the 1903 sculpture for the Wertheim department store in Berlin. The guidebook states that the sculpture was transferred to Burg Schlitz in 1930, which coincides with the Mosse family departure from Berlin. There is also a copy of the sculpture in Burlingame, California, known as the Wurlitzer Fountain, which the Wurlitzer family bought in Germany and placed initially in Cincinnati, Ohio.

47. BCCP, *Minutes* (Jan. 12, 1858), 131–32; Richard Hunter et al., Hunter Research, Inc., *A Preliminary Historical and Archeological Assessment to the North of the 97th Street Transverse Borough of Manhattan, City of New York,* vol. I, sect. 589–4, D 50–51; vol. II, illus. 59.

48. A letter from Gertrude Hall Brownell to DeWitt M. Lockman of the Municipal Arts Society, August 25, 1926, includes the proposed plan for "The Secret Garden" by landscape architect Charles Downing Lay; Central Park Conservancy files.

49. It had been abducted twice before, in 1963 and 1965, but immediately recovered. *New York Times,* Aug. 15, 1973, 41; Aug. 21, 1973, 12.

50. Sally Brown, *The Original Alice: From Manuscript to Wonderland* (London, undated). The fountain was moved from its original site adjacent to the Heckscher Playground to the James Michael Levin Playground in 1986.

51. Letter to the artist from George Delacorte, Sept. 19, 1957; letter from Stuart Constable to de Creeft, dated Feb. 2, 1958, in José de Creeft papers, Archives of American Art, reel D150#136, 1957.

52. Robert Smithson, "Frederick Law Olmsted and the Dialectical Landscape," *Artforum* (Feb. 1973): 68.

53. For further interpretation of the work see Suzaan Boettger, "A Found Weekend, 1967: Public Sculpture and Anti-Monuments," *Art in America* 89, no. 1 (Jan. 1, 2001): 80; see also, Barbara Haskell, *Claes Oldenburg: Object into Monument* (Pasadena, 1971), 61–62.

54. On March 26, 1981, the City Council adopted legislation introduced by council member Henry J. Stern on December 18, 1980, which designated this area as Strawberry Fields.

55. *New York Times,* Aug. 22, 1981, 48.

56. *New York Post,* Dec. 19, 1980.

57. BCCP, *Eighth Annual Report* (1864), 38. In his submission to the design competition, George Waring suggested a memorial to Downing.

Description of Plans, "Art the Handmaiden of Nature," no. 29, 81.

58. Related to the author in conversation on May 19, 2002 by M. M. Graff, who had visited Vaux's daughter, Marion Vaux Hendrickson, in a New York nursing home; see also *New York Herald,* Nov. 22, 1895. For a different opinion by Vaux's son Bowyer, see Kowsky, *Country, Park, and City,* 320.

59. *Forty Years,* note 4, 28.

60. FLO to CV, June 8, 1865, FLOP.

61. Alex Beam, *Gracefully Insane: The Rise and Fall of America's Premier Mental Hospital* (New York, 2001), 10. See also Witold Rybczynski, *A Clearing in the Distance* (New York, 1999), 406–11.

62. *Forty Years,* Appendix III, "The Facts in the Viele Case," 554–62; see also, BCCP, *Minutes* (Dec. 1, 1859), 195.

63. *Description of Plans,* "Presented as a design for the Park, but found to contain only a design for a pyramid," 1.

64. Peter Salwen, *Upper West Side Story* (New York, 1989), 65; see also Rebecca Read Shanor, *The City That Never Was* (New York, 1991), 86–90, 95–96, 177; Paul E. Cohen and Robert T. Augustyn, *Manhattan in Maps: 1527–1995* (New York, 1997), 130–31, 136–39.

65. Elizabeth Hawes, *New York, New York* (New York, 1993), 27–29.

66. *New York Times,* Nov. 27, 1872, 2.

More comprehensive endnotes to the text
can be found online:
www.centralparknyc.org
http://hometown.aol.com/svcm/saracedarmiller.html

Selected Bibliography

PRIMARY SOURCES

Board of Commissioners of the Central Park. *Annual Report of the Board of Commissioners of the Central Park.* New York, 1857–70.

_____. *Minutes of the Proceedings of the Board of Commissioners of the Central Park.* New York, 1857–70.

Board of Commissioners of the Department of Public Parks. *Annual Report of the Board of Commissioners of the Department of Public Parks.* New York, 1871–74, 1898–1931.

_____. *Minutes.* New York, 1871–98; some years unavailable.

Cook, Clarence. *A Description of the New York Central Park.* New York, 1869; rpt. New York, 1979.

Description of Plans for the Improvement of Central Park. New York, 1858.

Downing, Andrew Jackson. *Treatise on the Theory and Practice of Landscape Gardening.* New York, 1852.

MacLaughlin, Charles, ed. *The Papers of Frederick Law Olmsted.* Vols. 1–6; Supplementary Series, Vol. 1. Baltimore, 1977–1997.

Olmsted Jr., Frederick Law, and Theodora Kimball, eds. *Forty Years of Landscape Architecture: Central Park.* Cambridge, MA, 1973.

Parsons, Mabel, ed. *Memories of Samuel Parsons.* New York, 1926.

Perkins, Jr., Fred. B. and W. H. Guild. *The Central Park: Photographed with Descriptions and A Historical Sketch.* New York, 1864.

Ruskin, John, *Modern Painters.* Vols. 1–5. London, 1851–60.

_____. *The Seven Lamps of Architecture.* Rpt. of 2nd (1880) edition. New York: 1989.

_____. *The Stones of Venice.* Rpt. abridged 1860 edition. New York, 1985.

Tuckerman, Henry T. *Book of the Artists: American Artist.* New York, 1867.

Vaux, Calvert. *Villas and Cottages: A Series of Designs Prepared for Execution in the United States.* New York, 1857; 2nd edition 1864; rpt. New York, 1970.

[Wise, Daniel]. *Little Peachblossom: or Rambles in Central Park.* New York, 1873.

SECONDARY SOURCES

Alex, William. *Calvert Vaux: Architect & Planner.* New York, 1991.

Avery, Kevin. *Church's Great Picture: The Heart of the Andes.* New York, 1993.

Bender, Thomas. *New York Intellect: A History of Intellectual Life in New York City from 1750 to the Beginnings of Our Own Time.* Baltimore, 1987.

Beveridge, Charles E., and Paul Rocheleau. *Frederick Law Olmsted: Designing the American Landscape.* New York, 1995.

Bogart, Michele H. *Public Sculpture and the Civic Ideal in New York City, 1890–1930.* Washington, DC, 1997.

Burrows, Edwin G., and Mike Wallace. *Gotham: A History of New York City to 1898.* New York, 1999.

Craven, Wayne. *Sculpture in America.* Newark, DE, 1984.

Gayle, Margot, and Michele Cohen. *Guide to Manhattan's Outdoor Sculpture.* New York, 1988.

Gilmartin, Gregory F. *Shaping the City: New York and the Municipal Arts Society.* New York, 1995.

Gould, Stephen J. "Church, Humboldt, and Darwin: The Tension and Harmony of Art and Science." In Franklin Kelly, et al. *Frederick Edwin Church.* Washington, DC, 1989.

Graff, M. M. *Central Park, Prospect Park: A New Perspective.* New York, 1985.

Hall, Edward Hagaman. "Central Park in the City of New York." *Sixteenth Annual Report, American Scenic and Historic Preservation Society.* Albany, NY, 1911.

Kelly, Bruce, Travis Guillet, and Mary Ellen W. Hern. *Art of the Olmsted Landscape.* New York, 1981.

Koeppel, Gerard T. *Water for Gotham: A History.* Princeton, NJ, 2000.

Kouwenhoven, John. *Made in America.* New York, 1948; reprinted as *The Arts in Modern American Civilization.* New York, 1967.

Kowsky, Francis R. *Country, Park & City: The Architecture and Life of Calvert Vaux.* New York, 1998.

Marx, Leo. *The Machine in the Garden: Technology and the Pastoral Ideal in America.* New York, 1964.

McKay, Ernest A. *The Civil War and New York City.* Syracuse, NY, 1990.

Milroy, Elizabeth. "The Public Career of Emma Stebbins: Work in Marble." *Archives of American Art Journal* 33, no. 3 (1993): 2–12; "Work in Bronze." *Archives of American Art Journal* 34, no. 1 (1994): 2–13.

Miller, Angela. *The Empire of the Eye: Landscape Representation and American Cultural Politics, 1825–75.* Ithaca, 1993.

Novak, Barbara. *Nature and Culture: American Landscape and Painting 1825–1875.* New York, 1980.

Rogers, Elizabeth Barlow. *Landscape Design: A Cultural and Architectural History.* New York, 2002.

Roper, Laura Wood. FLO: *A Biography of Frederick Law Olmsted.* Baltimore, 1973; rpt. 1983.

Rosenzweig, Roy, and Elizabeth Blackmar. *The Park and the People.* Ithaca and London, 1992.

Schuyler, David. *Apostle of Taste: Andrew Jackson Downing, 1815–1852.* Baltimore and London, 1996.

_____. *The New Urban Landscape: The Redefinition of City Form in Nineteenth-Century America.* Baltimore and London, 1986.

Spann, Edward K. *The New Metropolis: New York City 1840–1857.* New York, 1981.

Upton, Dell. "Inventing the Metropolis." in *Art and the Empire City: New York, 1825–1861.* New York, 2000, 2–45.

Van Zanten, David T. "Jacob Wrey Mould: Echoes of Owen Jones and the High Victorian Styles in New York, 1853–1865." *Journal of the Society of Architectural Historians* 28 (1969): 41–57.

A complete bibliography is accessible on the following websites:
www.centralparknyc.org
http://hometown.aol.com/svcm/saracedarmiller.html

One criterion used to critique a great work of art is its longevity—the ability to initiate emotion and communicate meaning long after it was created. In this sense, Central Park is a masterpiece that has survived the test of time.

Like any great work of art, the Park requires a great deal of care to maintain its beauty and energy. For more than twenty years the Central Park Conservancy has been engaged in that care, working to restore and preserve Central Park for the 25 million individuals who visit the Park each year. The Conservancy, a private nonprofit organization, daily tends to the many tasks needed to keep the Park the magnificent oasis that it remains today. Our staff members plant the flowers, mow the lawns, rake the leaves, shovel the snow, repair the benches, pick up the litter, provide the tours, operate the visitor centers, oversee the playgrounds, and handle the many unseen challenges presented in caring for a living, manmade masterpiece of 843 acres located in the middle of the world's greatest city. Since 1998, when it entered into a contract with the City of New York, the Central Park Conservancy has been designated "keeper of the park," officially responsible for its ongoing maintenance and operation. The cost of all this, however, amounts to nearly $20 million each year, 85 percent of which must be raised by the Conservancy from generous individuals, foundations, and corporations.

Sara Cedar Miller, through her beautiful and artistic images, has chronicled the Conservancy's work to preserve the original vision of Olmsted and Vaux. In these pages her passion for the Park is palpable, inspiring and reminding each of us how significant the Park is to our lives. But the Park is also our responsibility. Protecting and preserving Central Park is a noble work. I hope you will join us in that effort.

REGINA S. PERUGGI
PRESIDENT
CENTRAL PARK CONSERVANCY

The mission of the Central Park Conservancy is to restore, manage, and preserve Central Park, in partnership with the public, for the enjoyment of current and future generations. Since its founding in 1980, the Conservancy has developed and implemented a major management and restoration plan, performed major capital improvements, created programs for volunteers and visitors, and set new standards of excellence in Park care; it is in the process of building an endowment to ensure continued Park maintenance.

Acknowledgments

For nearly two decades it has been my privilege to capture Central Park's glorious restoration on film. Yes, I had the joy of taking the photographs, but I did not do the work that each image represents. That credit goes to my colleagues at the Central Park Conservancy, the men and women who have contributed in so many different ways to restoring and maintaining this important work of art. This dedicated team includes the board of trustees and the members of the women's committee, planners, landscape architects, horticulturists, artists, artisans, fund raisers, educators, finance and administrative staff, and our municipal partners, the New York City Department of Parks & Recreation. Above all, I want to acknowledge the generosity of the donors and volunteers who have given unstintingly of their time, money, effort, and care to make this renaissance possible. In a very real sense, this book is their creation.

Most authors are lucky to have had a single mentor. I am blessed with two. I spent my seminal years in the graduate art history department of Hunter College with Leo Steinberg, whose original work was the guiding spirit during the research and writing of this book. Thanks to Cynthia Larson, I met Betsy Barlow Rogers who gave me the job of a lifetime. She opened my eyes to the history and meaning of landscape in general and Central Park in particular. Her passion has been my inspiration.

As my ideas developed about the history of the Park and its features, many people acted as sounding boards and critics. Charles Beveridge, Olmsted Papers, American University and Frank Kowsky,

Buffalo State College, read the entire manuscript. Kevin Avery of the Metropolitan Museum of Art, Michele Bogart of the State University of New York at Stony Brook, Jonathan Kuhn of the New York City Department of Parks, and historians Rebecca Shanor, Deborah Epstein Solon, and Karen Zukowski have also contributed important comments. Historians Bill Alex, Elizabeth Blackmar, Ethan Carr, M. M. Graff, Barry Lewis, Elizabeth Milroy, Roy Rosenzweig, David Schuyler, and Eric Washington have also given valuable information and advice over the years.

My colleagues at the Conservancy and Parks contributed ideas, opinions, and visual assistance for the past eighteen years. Regrettably, limited space makes it impossible to name them all, though I feel I must mention: Regina Alvarez, Sally Austin, Bill Berliner, Doug Blonsky, Dennis Burton, Neil Calvanese, Peter Champe, Marianne Cramer, Gary Dearborn, Nicole Buchwalter Fox, Tom Giordano, Judith Heintz, Maria Hernandez, Lorraine Konopka, Richard Kruzansky, David Landreth, Tim Marshall, Patricia McCobb, Charles McKinney, Lawrence Mauro, Lynden Miller, Sal Napolitano, Chris Nolan, Kathy Palmer, Jeff Poor, Sarah Price, David Robinson, Diane Schaub, Lauren Stahl, Mark Rabinowitz, Marie Ruby, Frank Serpe, Laura Starr, Laurie Weisman, and the late Bruce Kelly and Phil Winslow. The text is immeasurably better for their input and expertise.

I did not come to writing easily. Friends and colleagues have all patiently parsed my words—in many instances improving my words with their own. I learned the art of writing and assembling a book proposal from Charles Kipps and Jack Freiberg, both long-time friends and faithful supporters of this project. Eve Rothenberg and Alice Baer

have guided me through the nuances of the English language. Lane Addonizio, Richard Burgheim, Michelle Eldredge, Kevin Kiddoo, Frank Kowsky, Chris Nolan, Rita Powell, Rebecca Shanor, and Deborah Solon brought their editorial skills to the text as well as important suggestions about the book's organization.

Michael and Stephen Cohen and the staff at New York Film Works have been my professional lifeline and my good friends. Herbert Mitchell and his collection of Central Park photographs were instrumental to my research. The collection of Central Park drawings and city archives were made accessible to me for study by Ken Cobb, Director of the Municipal Archives, Evelyn Gonzales, who catalogued the drawings, and Laura McCann, Meghan Goldmann, Mirah von Wicht, and Ellen Chin, who restored the Rink watercolor for publication and exhibition.

I am most grateful to Marian Heilbrun and her library staff and President Kenneth Jackson, Cynthia Copeland, and former staff members Grady Turner and Stewart Desmond of the New-York Historical Society, where most of this research took place; President David McKinney, Kevin Avery, Kay Bearman, and Morrison Heckscher at the Metropolitan Museum of Art; Sidney Horenstein and Niles Eldridge of the American Museum of Natural History; Thomas Savini, Chancellor Robert R. Livingston Library and Museum; Jonathan Harding of The Century Association; Liz Good of the New Orleans Pharmacy Museum; Tupper Thomas and her staff at Prospect Park; Steve Miscenzik at the Cleveland Museum of Natural History; M. P. Naud and Joe Goddu at Hirschl & Adler Galleries; Evelyn Trebilcock at Olana State Historic Site;

Wendy Hurlock at the Archives of American Art; Deborah Bershad at the Art Commission; Richard Hunter and Lynn Rakos of Hunter Research, Inc.; artists Christo and Jeanne-Claude; Mary Daniels of Loeb Library, Harvard University; Jonathan Kuhn and his staff in the Department of Arts and Antiquities of New York City Parks; and last of all, the four Park Commissioners who have been so helpful to me over the years: Gordon Davis, Henry J. Stern, Betsy Gotbaum, and Adrian Benepe; and the four chairmen of the Central Park Conservancy: Bill Beineke, Jim Evans, Ira Millstein, and Ian Smith. I want to thank the many committee members of the 150th anniversary committees, as well as Eleanora Kennedy, Gail Hilson, Betty Sherill, and the entire Tree Trust committee for the exhibition of my photographs. I am grateful to many people who have generously opened their homes or offices for photographing the Park: Barbara and Kirk Browning, Richard Burgheim, Ted and Jane Koryn, Ira Millstein, Julian and Josie Robertson, Susan and Jack Rudin, Michael and Elizabeth Varet, Dolores Velez, Bob Wilson, the Metropolitan Museum of Art; Mt. Sinai Hospital, Trump International, the El Dorado, and the Terence Cardinal Cooke Health Care Center.

Writing is a lonely business and trying to get published is even harder; a personal support system makes all the difference. Roberta Bernstein, more a sister than a friend for more than forty years, instilled the passion for learning and art that has been the foundation of my life. Phyllis Cohen helped me to believe in myself and to believe in the possibility of the project. Charles Kipps taught me to never give up. Laura Starr and Zeke Berman, Cheryl Best and Sarah Maslanka, Debi Best and Eric Parker, Barry, Ed and Sue Cedar, Michelle and Niles Eldredge, Jack Freiberg, Judith Heintz, Andrea Hill, Kevin Kiddoo, Frederic Lillien, David Miller, Viki Sand, the late Eloise Segal, Rebecca Shanor, Susan Urban, Asha Weinstein, and most of all my daughter Alison Miller have cared for me and nurtured me during both good and difficult times. At the Conservancy and Parks I have had wonderful support from Elaine Adley, Claude Barrileaux, Ed Benson, Myra Biblowit, Jill Bristow, Samantha Burwick, Pamela Butler, Tia Chapman, Jesse Cohen, Ronise Cox, Mary Cregg, Pat De Bary, Joyce Ferejohn, Sharon Flescher, Russell Fredericks, Dina Freidman, Renee Friedman, Kate French, Cathy Grupper, Ann Hagen, Lennox Hannan, Chip Horton, Margaret Hunt, Adam Kaufman, Nancy Kelly, Jeanne Kim, Cornelia Knight, Risa Korris, Clare McCarthy, Al McMorris, Mindy Miller, Nelson Nicholas, Marcy O'Dell, Ken Olshan, Betsy Pugh, Jim Reed, Chris Seita, Norma Soto, Susan Stanton, Erana Stenett, Shawn Taylor, Lydia Thomas, Pam Tice, Kay Toll, Louis Urrutia-Orme, Elizabeth Varet, Jennifer Wald, Paola Zanzo, and the late and great Joan Frank.

Last of all, I want to thank the people who made this book a reality. Betsy Rogers put in the good word for me at Abrams. John Crowley, former manager of rights and reproductions, believed in the project from the beginning, and Eric Himmel has been a tremendous supporter. My editor at Abrams, Elisa Urbanelli, herself a sensitive art historian, brought a tough critical intelligence to the ideas, a style and grace that immeasurably improved the final text, and a brilliance at orchestrating my vision into this final work. I watched the book evolve into a beautiful work of art under the discerning eye and impeccable taste of talented designer Bob McKee, who kept his good nature and sense of humor through hundreds of changes, revisions, and artistic decisions. I am grateful to Conservancy President Regina Peruggi, who approved the text as well as additional artwork that contributed to the book's uniqueness and elegance. I am grateful to Ira Millstein, Ken Heitner, and Bernadette McCann Ezrin of Weil, Gotshal, and Manges, who donated their legal services and expertise to both the Conservancy and to me, and to Steve Spinelli, Vice President of Finance, who spearheaded the business aspects of the project and, with Regina Peruggi, showed me extreme generosity and respect. I wish also to thank Belinda Adefioye and Alicea Paez for their assistance with the permissions process. Former Vice President of Development Vin Spinelli gave the nod to staff members Sarah Himmelfarb and Ellen Goldstein to secure the necessary funding. Most of all, I am profoundly grateful to Chief Operating Officer and Central Park Administrator Doug Blonsky. By believing in my work and my vision, he made this book possible.

The Al and Trudy Kallis Foundation were early supporters of the project. Their gift made color reproduction of the paintings in the book possible.

THE HENRY LUCE
FOUNDATION

*The Central Park
Conservancy is grateful
to the foundation for its
generous support of this book.*

Index

Truman, Harry S., 164
Turtle Pond, *118*
Tweed administration, 171, 173, 174, 175, 181–82,
  186, 234

U
Ugly Duckling, 222, *223*
Umpire Rock, *96*
Untermyer, Samuel, 220
Untermyer Fountain (Schott), 220, *220*
U.S.S. *Maine,* 208

V
Vanderbilt, Cornelius II, 209
Vaux, Calvert, *74,* 233; and arches and bridges,
  103; as architect, 156–57, 159, 161, 162, 167, 168,
  170, 173, 178, 185; as artist, 9; and Bethesda
  Terrace, 34, 36–37, 39, 41, 42–44, 49, 53, 55, 56,
  63, 64, 66, 68, 97; democratic ideas of, 28, 95,
  239; and Downing, 18, 25, 74–75, 173; and
  Garden Arcade, 97; and gates, 56–57, 201;

influences on, 43–44, 68, 76, 88; and initial
  park plans, 75; and the Mall, 59, 60, 61; and
  Mould, 37, 41, 61, 64, 178, 185; and Olmsted,
  see Olmsted and Vaux; other parks designed
  by, 231, 233, 238; resignation of, 56, 57; and
  sculpture, 191, 202; and Venetian Gothic shel-
  ter, *96; Villas and Cottages* by, 156
Vaux, Downing, 231
Vaux, Mary McEntee, 75
Venetian Gothic shelter, 95, *96*
Viele, Egbert Ludovicus, 75, 77, 233–34; early
  plan of, *77,* 79, 81, *82,* 234
Villas and Cottages (Vaux), 156
Vista Rock, 33, *55,* 77, 162
Vonnoh, Bessie Potter, *Burnett Fountain,* 221, *221*
Voyage of Life, Childhood (Cole), 44, *44*

W
Wagner Cove, *123*
Ward, John Quincy Adams, 192–95; *Indian
  Hunter,* 192–93, *192, 193,* 195, 206; *The Pilgrim,*

22, 196, *196–97; Seventh Regiment Memorial,*
  22, 202–3, *202; Shakespeare,* 192, *194,* 195
Waring, George, 80, 81; plan by, *85,* 146
War of 1812, 164
water, *12,* 119–27; cascades, *138, 139;*
  Conservatory Water, 146, *146, 147;* fountains,
  27, *154–55,* 209, 220, 221, *221,* 222, 224, *224;*
  Harlem Meer, 126, *126–27;* healing properties
  of, 64, 65, 66, 161; importance of, 88; reservoirs,
  26, *26, 78, 79,* 100, 116, *118,* 198; *see also* Lake,
  the; Loch, the; Pond, the; Pool, the; Turtle Pond
Weather Service, U.S., 162, 179
Webster, Daniel, 22, 196–97, *196*
William Tecumseh Sherman (Saint-Gaudens), 22,
  22, 204, *205,* 206
Withers, Frederick Clarke, 96
Wollman Skating Rink, *125*
woodlands, *see* trees

Z
Zoo, 180, *180,* 182

255

Editor: Elisa Urbanelli
Designer: Robert McKee
Production Manager: Maria Pia Gramaglia

Library of Congress Cataloging-in-Publication Data

Miller, Sara Cedar.
Central Park, an American masterpiece :
a comprehensive history of the nation's first urban
park / text and photographs by Sara Cedar Miller.
  p. cm.
Includes bibliographical references and index.
  ISBN 0-8109-3946-0 (hardcover)
1. Central Park (New York, N.Y.)—History. 2.
Central Park (New York, N.Y.)—Pictorial works. 3.
New York (N.Y.)—Description and travel. I. Central
Park Conservancy (New York, N.Y.) II. Title.

F128.65.C3 M55 2003
712'.5'097471—dc21
                    2002151491

Harry N. Abrams, Inc.
100 Fifth Avenue
New York, N.Y. 10011
www.abramsbooks.com

Abrams is a subsidiary of